THE EINSTEIN SYNDROME

Corporate Anti-Semitism in America Today

Stephen L. Slavin
Mary A. Pradt

UNIVERSITY
PRESS OF
AMERICA

University Press of America, Inc."

P.O. Box 19101, Washington, D.C. 20036

Printed in the United States of America

Library of Congress Cataloging in Publication Data

Slavin, Stephen L.
   The Einstein syndrome.

   Includes bibliographical references.
   1. Antisemitism--United States. 2. Jews--United
States--Employment. 3. Discrimination in employment--
United States. 4. United States--Ethnic relations.
I. Pradt, Mary A. II. Title.
DS146.U6S53   305.8'924'073   81-43767
ISBN 0-8191-2370-6   AACR2
ISBN 0-8191-2371-4 (pbk.)

ACKNOWLEDGEMENTS

Our work on this book was aided by literally hundreds of people -- college and corporate officers, executive recruiters, officials of the American Jewish Congress, Anti-Defamation League, American Jewish Committee, and the Civil Rights Division of the New York State Attorney General's Office, as well as the editors of the journals which published our articles. Rather than try to name everyone , we'll name no one.

TABLE OF CONTENTS

PREFACE

Over the last few years we have collaborated on three articles on corporate anti-Semitism, which appeared in Jewish Currents, the Jewish Spectator, and The Bankers Magazine. Parts of these articles are reprinted here along with a considerable array of additional data.

There is really no question that there is anti-Semitism in Corporate America today, but only the degree to which it exists. We have tried to show that it continues to be a major problem. Our perspective is that American Jews are not fully accepted, particularly in the upper echelons of the corporate hierarchy. Although individual Jews have "made it," we have tried to show that Jewish executives are systematically excluded from the corporate mainstream

CHAPTER I.   INTRODUCTION

We are living in the era of revolution. Racial
and sexual equality have become theoretically acceptable to most Americans, although only minimal progress
has been made in real terms. Wounded Knee and Selma,
Alabama are familiar places. Italo-Americans have
insisted that they too, are victims, even going so far
as to emulate the Jewish Anti-Defamation League. Whatever the final outcome of these revolutions, America
will never be the same.

It would be quite within the spirit of the times
for Jews to protest not just 300 years of oppression,
but 2,000 or more, depending on when you start counting.
But since Jews are apparently doing quite well eco-
nomically, perhaps they should just count their
blessings and thank God to be living in the land of
opportunity.

In our interviews with Jewish corporate executives, we came across a very ambiguous attitude. While
many claimed to have encountered little anti-Semitism,
they questioned the wisdom of writing a book which
might stir "them" up. The ever-present anti-Semites,
just waiting for an excuse to pounce, could, at any

time, snatch away all the gains of the last two generations.

There is no question that Jews are doing well, but we must ask if they could do still better. Perhaps more important, we must ask if Jews are being steered into "Jewish jobs," and systematically excluded from those in the corporate mainstream. Obviously, that is our contention.

Why is it that there are so many Jews in certain fields -- retailing, the movies, publishing, network television, apparel, and textiles -- while there are so few in banking, the public utilities, and heavy industry? We will consider this question throughout the book, on the basis of college recruitment data, personal interviews, the responses to our surveys, and analysis of corporate promotion patterns. Each Jewish college graduate might ask himself, "Am I avoiding them, or are they avoiding me?"

The position taken here is that, contrary to popular belief, there is still a substantial amount of discrimination against Jews in large corporations. We have found that nearly all large corporations a) do not send recruiters to schools with large Jewish enrollments; b) do not hire Jewish graduates of the schools with lower Jewish enrollments; and c) do not hire Jews through employment agencies. The few Jews permitted to work for these firms are restricted largely to a few specialized departments such as data processing, legal, or sales. It has also been found that hundreds of other large companies, although perhaps not actively anti-Semitic, each have only a few Jewish executives out of several thousand.

This is a book about Jews who are trying to assimilate -- like the German Jews did before them. It is also about the efforts of the WASPs in charge to keep their banks and their oil companies, and their other huge corporations staffed by WASPs and WASP types in perpetuity.

Imagine a company that hired whites only, but did allow blacks who looked white to work there. Light-skinned blacks, if so inclined, would be welcome as long as they could "pass." For years Jews have also been "passing."

Of course it is a lot easier for Jews to get away with this ploy than blacks. Often a change of name and nose will do the trick. Even so, only a small

2

minority of Jews prove to be willing and able to pass the WASP test.

A second way of finding gainful employment in the corporate world is to have a specialty that is in demand. A very high proportion of data processing jobs is held by Jews -- and Orientals, for that matter. Accounting positions, as well as those in law, personnel, public relations, economic analysis, and other highly technical fields, are also staffed largely by Jews. In fact, in few large corporations can one find Jews in anything other than these specialized staff positions? There is one exception, however -- sales. Especially when the customers happen to be Jewish.

We call this phenomenon of placing Jews in "Jewish jobs" the "Einstein Syndrome." At first glance this may not be an entirely bad thing since these jobs are usually well-paying and certainly not demeaning like "women's work" or "nigger's work." Surely it is better to be a JPA (Jewish Public Accountant) or a computer programmer than a nurse, secretary, domestic worker, or janitor. It's hard to understand that it is demeaning to be slotted for any job whether on the basis of race, sex, or religion. The corporate official who hires a "smart Jewish lawyer" is just as bad as the one who looks for a "pretty secretary."

One way out is to change your name -- and somehow escape the stigma of being Jewish. Moscowitz becomes Morse, Weinstein, Winston or Winters, and Berkowitz, Burke.[2] But as sociologist Paul Esposito has remarked, "No WASP ever ethnicized his name."

This study is not meant to make light of the discrimination faced by blacks, women, Italian-Americans, Hispanics, or any other group. Sometimes, when a black person complains about his difficulties getting a decent job, his third-generation American friend tells him, "My parents had it hard too." This specious reasoning is unworthy of comment. Many people dismiss Jewish complaints about employment discrimination with similar disdain. "How can you say you're discriminated against? You run practically everything!" It seems to many Americans that half our vocabulary is Yiddish; contributing to the language, however, is not a measure of real economic power.

It is generally accepted that blacks and women are excluded from most well-paying jobs and are crowded

3

into less desirable occupations.[3] If we can show that Jews too, are not allowed to work in certain industries, then one might well wonder where this process ends. Is there an allocation of jobs not only on the basis of race and sex, but also by religious and ethnic group? To what degree, then, is our economy misallocating its labor and consequently operating at less than full efficiency? And how equitable is a society that places economic sanctions on individuals merely because they were somewhat careless about picking their ancestors?

If America is indeed still discriminating against Jews, it would be a pretty fair assumption that several other groups might be getting the short end of the stick. While this investigation focuses on the treatment of Jews by large corporations, any adverse conclusions might well be also applicable to blacks, Hispanics, and women on a much larger scale.

The main hypothesis of this study may be stated as three related propositions: (1) That very few major corporations recruit at colleges with large Jewish enrollments; (2) that most major corporations hire relatively few Jews, given the availability of Jewish college graduates; and (3) that virtually all of those Jews hired are placed in "Jewish jobs."

So why write a book about one of the most affluent groups in America? It is difficult to perceive a relatively well-to-do segment of our population as being oppressed. Unless this seeming paradox is resolved, it would be difficult for the reader to accept the evidence of employment discrimination that is presented in subsequent chapters. In the next chapter, then, we will attempt to resolve this paradox.

Chapter Notes

1. About 2.7% of the U.S. population is Jewish. See the American Jewish Year Book 1981 (New York: The American Jewish Committee and the Jewish Publication Society of America, 1981), p. 173.

2. See Appendix, Section C, for differentiation between Jewish and Christian names.

3. The crowding hypothesis, which was expounded by Daniel Fusfeld (The Basic Economics of the Urban Racial Crisis, New York: Holt, Rinehart and Winston, 1973) has been used to explain how blacks are made to do society's dirty work and to do it for very little pay. We merely exclude blacks from all the jobs that whites want, so that blacks really are left with little choice.

CHAPTER II.   THE AMBIGUOUS AFFLUENCE OF AMERICAN JEWS

> "Remember, we must be twice as good
> to get half as much."
> > Heinrich Heine

> "The first Jewish President will be
> an Episcopalian."
> > Harry Golden

A.   Introduction

Most Americans, and probably most Jews as well,
would deny that anti-Semitism is still a powerful
force. Jewish Supreme Court Justices, Senators, and
even a Jewish Secretary of State belie such con-
tentions. The movies are Jewish and every other author
has a Jewish name, or once did. Macys is Jewish,
Gimbels is Jewish, and so are many other department
stores throughout the land.

The Jewish presence or dominance in certain fields
is well-known: retailing, the movies, publishing, the

7

t.v. networks, as well as apparel and textiles are Jewish preserves. On the other hand, not many people are aware that there are very few Jews in banking, the public utilities, heavy industry (most notably oil, autos, and steel) and transportation. Of course, there are only so many Jews to go around, so if they are concentrated in the former group of industries, there won't be enough Jews to work in the latter. One question which suggests itself is whether so many Jews are in the first group because they chose to be, or because they were excluded from the second group.

"Would you believe that less than two per cent of all bank executives in New York City are Jewish?"

"Are you kidding?"

"That's right. And that only one out of every two hundred officers of the top fifty public utilities is Jewish?"

"Go on! In this day and age!"

"Listen, in this day and age nearly all the large corporations still avoid recruiting at colleges with substantial Jewish enrollments."

For the last two years we have been researching and writing a book on corporate anti-Semitism. In interviewing and discussing the subject with many people, the same question kept recurring -- Are Jews still being discriminated against in this day and age? Others told us we were beating a dead horse. We felt it necessary to resolve this paradox -- how a seemingly affluent group could be the object of discrimination. Jews, after all, are the most affluent group in America.

The admitted affluence of the American Jewish population must be seen in context. How many of them are there, how rich are they, and how much power do they really wield? The stereotype would be easy to delineate. Jews have carved out their slice of the pie, but how big is it? What are those six million people, representing 2.7% of the total U.S. population, doing out there?

B. The Jewish Population of the United States

Data on size, location, income and educational attainment of Jews help explain how this relatively well-to-do segment of our population is still oppressed. Unless we can explain Jews' relatively high incomes, even the most open-minded reader would find it hard to believe that this group still faces employment discrimination. In fact, taking into account their socioeconomic status -- especially urban residence and level of education -- Jews have earnings comparable to those of their non-Jewish peers. Although they make the same money, Jews make it in different places. This aspect of discrimination is most evident among Jewish college graduates. It is they who take relatively unpleasant and low-status jobs compared to their gentile counterparts' positions.

The distribution of the American Jewish population is extremely uneven. Nearly as many Jews live in New York and California as in all the other 48 states combined.

The eight states that have fairly large Jewish populations cast nearly forty per cent of the votes in the electoral college. This factor may explain the importance of the Jewish vote in presidential elections.

Not only is the American Jewish population concentrated in large industrial states, but it is centered in heavily urban areas in these states.

Over 68 per cent of all Jews live in cities of one million or more, compared with about 30 per cent of Catholics and 10 per cent of Protestants.[1] Jews have relatively high incomes simply because people living in urban areas tend to be more prosperous than those living in rural areas.[2] Furthermore, nearly all of America's large industrial and financial corporations have headquarters in close proximity to New York, Los Angeles, Philadelphia, Chicago and other large cities. The Jewish population would appear to be conveniently located for employment in the corporate sector. Although under three per cent of the U.S. population is Jewish, Jews would seem to be an obvious source for corporate recruiters.

In the mid-sixties Gallup polls indicated that more than 71 per cent of all Jews aged thirty and over

TABLE I

Jewish Population in Selected States
(Estimated), 1980

State	Total Population	Estimated Jewish Population
California...........	22,694,000	753,945
Florida	8,860,000	454,880
Illinois	11,229,000	266,385
Maryland	4,148,000	185,915
Massachusetts	5,769,000	249,455
New Jersey	7,332,000	442,765
New York	17,648,000 2,140,690
Pennsylvania	11,731,000	419,730
TOTAL, U.S. 220,099,000		5,920,890

Source: American Jewish Yearbook, 1981 (New York:
The American Jewish Committee and Philadelphia: The
Jewish Publication Society of America, 1981, pp. 172 -
173.

TABLE II

Largest Jewish Communities in the U.S.
(Estimated), 1980

City	Jewish Population
New York City	1,228,000
Greater New York	1,998,000
Metropolitan Los Angeles	503,000
Metropolitan Philadelphia	295,000
Metropolitan Chicago	253,000
Miami	225,000
Boston	170,000
Greater Washington, D.C.	160,000
Bergen County, N.J.	100,000
Essex County area, N.J.	95,000
Baltimore	92,000
Cleveland	75,000
Detroit	75,000
San Francisco	75,000
Fort Lauderdale, Florida	75,000
St. Louis	60,000

Source: American Jewish Yearbook, 1981 (New York: The American Jewish Committee and Philadelphia: The Jewish Publication Society of America, 1981), pp. 175 - 182.

were high school graduates compared to about 47 per cent of the total white population. Over 20 per cent of the Jews were also college graduates, while less than 10 per cent of the total white population had a college degree.[3] The relatively high educational attainment of the Jews would indicate a greater likelihood of corporate employment. Data collected in this study prove the opposite has occurred.

There is some evidence of qualitative differences between the college education received by Jews, compared with other population groups. Also, a disproportionate number of Jewish college graduates go for graduate or professional training.[4] Approximately 20 per cent of students at the Ivy League schools are Jewish (See Appendix A). It's likely, furthermore, that the percentage of Jewish students at these and other leading colleges would be even higher were it not for regional quotas.[5] While 10 per cent of all college graduates are Jewish, much higher percentages of doctors, lawyers, and college teachers are Jewish.[6] Therefore, we have probably underestimated the true educational differential between Jews and the rest of the population.

C. The Affluence of American Jews

The popular belief that Jews are relatively affluent is borne out by available data. Table III provides a breakdown of income levels by religion. Jews are clearly better off as a group than are Catholics or Protestants, most notably with respect to representation in the upper income group.

Recent data are hard to obtain. Since the mid-Sixties, minorities have been increasingly reluctant to reveal their identification (whether racial, religious, ethnic, or even sexual). The pattern of Jews' income and employment does not, however, appear to have changed radically.

Nathan Glazer and Daniel Moynihan illustrated the difficulty of obtaining this type of data:

> ...a Jew always eagerly asks, in any situation, "How many are Jews?" And when he gets an answer, he asks suspiciously, "How do you know?"[7]

TABLE III

Relative Affluence of Protestants,
Catholics, and Jews, 1963 - 1964

Income	Protestants	Catholics	Jews
Lower (under $10,500)*	64.1%	59.0%	42.0%
Middle ($10,500 - 22,500)	30.9%	37.6%	48.8%
Upper ($22,500 & over)	5.0%	3.4%	9.2%
	100.0%	100.0%	100.0%

* The dollar figures from Glenn and Hyland have been tripled to reflect the fact that both wages and the Consumer Price Index have tripled since 1964.

Source: Norval D. Glenn and Ruth Hyland, "Religious Preference and Worldly Success: Some Evidence from National Surveys." American Sociological Review, Vol. 35, February 1965.

Although, as our findings will demonstrate, Jews are still excluded from certain jobs, they don't appear to be the worse for it. How much exclusion can possibly be taking place if Jewish incomes are so high? A reasonable observer might conclude that if there is employment discrimination, it cannot be very widespread and Jewish incomes do not suffer greatly as a result. If these crucial points were not satisfactorialy explained, this issue would be academic and this book irrelevant. Here we must resolve the seeming contradiction -- that Jews are affluent, yet simultaneously oppressed. Once we inspect the data and realize that Jewish incomes are no higher than might be expected for any group with certain social characteristics, we can deal more freely with the issue of employment discrimination.

Two key social characteristics, as we noted earlier, set Jews apart from other groups. Jews are not only the most highly urbanized group in America, but also have the highest educational attainment. If a person in Jewish, it is more than six times as likely that he lives in a large city than if he were Protestant. Similarly, it is nearly three times as likely that he is a college graduate.

Not only do Jewish families almost universally pack their children (especially sons) off to college, they push them on to graduate and professional school as well. Since income is directly proportional to years of schooling, it is not surprising that Jews, perhaps two-thirds of whom are college graduates, happen to earn the incomes of college graduates.[8] The relationship between urban residence and income is also well-documented. In the U.S. there has long been a substantial income differential between urban and rural dwellers.[9] Because Jews reside almost entirely in urban areas, they are in an excellent position to benefit from this differential.[10]

Jewish money is very "new" money, because it was made only one or two generations ago, rather than the requisite three or four. Jews began arriving here in large numbers around the turn of the century, but their economic ascent has been faster than that of any other immigrant group. Can this rise be traced to a decline in anti-Semitism? Surely not in the Thirties and Forties. Overt anti-Semitism markedly declined since then, but the urban residence and high educational attainment of Jews has been the most crucial factor in their climb to affluence.

Are Jews' relatively high incomes, then, merely reflections of their residential and educational characteristics? Several studies have concluded that when the incomes of Jews are compared to those of other groups with the same characteristics of residence and education, the income differential disappears.[11] Educated urbanites have relatively high earnings, so Jews are earning about what they might be expected to earn. But Jewish incomes would be still higher if Jews were not still excluded from many well paying jobs in the corporate sector.

The persistence of employment discrimination is also reflected by the type of jobs allocated to Jews. Traditionally, most societies assign their dirty work, most unpleasant tasks, and lowest status jobs to oppressed minorities. There are still substantial numbers of Jews in the working class (such as garment workers, postal employees, cab drivers and typists). The hierarchical politics of dirty work extend to the jobs held by college educated people. Of all positions available to college graduates, the least desirable are reserved for minorities, including Jews.

D.   Jews as an Outsider Group[12]

Thorstein Veblen, a penetrating social observer, saw the Jew in Europe after World War I both as a member of his society and as an outsider.[13]   Never fully accepted, he was still a citizen of his country. The Jew was able to participate, yet retain his objectivity and scientific skepticism.   The high proportion of Jewish scientists and writers throughout the world lends much credence to Veblen's thesis.

Three other groups play roles socioeconomically analogous to that of American Jews.   The overseas Chinese have done extremely well in commerce and the professions.   In Cuba, Vietnam, Indonesia, elsewhere in Southeast Asia, and even the United States, this group has prospered.   One would be hardput to explain the affluence of the Chinese-Americans, given the discrimination they have faced.

The Indians and Pakistanis have fared well in East Africa, Great Britain, the Caribbean, and the

United States -- largely as merchants. Like the
Chinese and the Jews, they started with little or no
capital and quickly built up prosperous, family-run
businesses.

A third group, the Palestinians, are known,
ironically enough, as "the Jews of the Arab world."
Without a homeland since the creation of Israel and
Jordan, a majority of the three million Palestinians
are not refugees in tents but college-trained technicians and executives employed throughout the Middle
East. They are also far more prosperous than the
average citizens of their host nations.

Jews and members of these three outsider groups
have five traits in common. Each is a recent immigrant
group. All are ethnically distinct from a majority
of people in their adopted land. They tend to live
in an urban environment and be relatively well-edu-
cated. All are relatively affluent. Each is viewed
with some hostility by his fellow citizens.

The affluence of outsider groups -- the American
Jews, overseas Chinese, Indians, Pakistanis, and
Palestinians -- has been attained despite the hard-
ships of immigration and discrimination. If we apply
Veblen's thesis, we would infer that each of these
immigrant minorities was able to maintain sufficient
objectivity and skepticism to overcome the inertia and
traditions of their adopted lands.

E. How Jews "Made It" in America

Most Jewish immigrants arrived at Ellis Island
penniless, refugees from Czarist pogroms. Many barely
assimilated. At first relegated to ghettos, they
often remained there voluntarily, retaining Yiddish
as their language. These Jews mainly worked in the
garment trade, just as they had in Europe. Those who
adapted more quickly became businessmen, albeit on a
small scale at first.

          Why did so many immigrant boys
      and men take to peddling? Probably
      it was the quickest way to get started
      in America.... And he could start the
      day after he got off the boat. Upon
      arrival at the dock he went to the

home of a friend or relative, ate
supper and gossiped for three hours,
then got a good night's sleep. The
next morning he went out and borrowed
forty dollars from a different friend
or relative and went down to the
wholesale district. There be bought
forty dollars' worth of sheets,
pillowcases, and blankets and started
walking toward New Jersey. A week
later he was able to buy sixty-two
dollars' worth.[14]

Of course, the Jewish immigrant had a special
incentive to go into business for himself -- no one
else would hire him. Luckily, the first three decades
of this century were a time of rapid economic ex-
pansion, of brand new industries, and perhaps most
important for the Jews, it didn't take much capital
to set up a business.

Excluded from established business, Jews were
forced to start their own. They gambled on the embry-
onic fields that were beginning to emerge. Revson
started with nail polish, Sarnoff (RCA) and Paley
(CBS) with commercial radio, while Jews built Hollywood
from scratch. "The men who built the motion picture
industry (Fox, Laemmle, Zukor, Selig, Loew, Goldwyn,
Lasky, Warner, Mayer) were not drawn from the supposedly farsighted ranks of American business. They
came, instead, from the marginal and shabby zones of
enterprise, from vaudeville, nickelodeon parlors,[15]
theatrical agencies, flea circuses, petty trade."
So maybe the anti-Semitic establishment really did the
Jews a favor by forcing them to start their own
firms.

Professor Feliks Gross has noted that the Jews
are accepted in a society in which they provide comple-
mentary services, somewhat peripheral to the economic
mainstream, but nevertheless useful. However, when
the Jews become competitive, they are no longer toler-
ated. The German example is easily recalled: the Jews
thought of themselves as Germans, but the Germans
thought otherwise. The Jews made the mistake of
competing.

This mistake has been avoided by American Jews,

although the choice was not theirs. The biggest
economic opportunities for Jews have always been the
newest or most exotic industries -- movies, publishing,
television, computers. You don't find Jews pushing
their way into most industrial sectors because you
can't get to the top by starting your own auto firm,
steel mill, or airline. You have to work your way up
the corporate ladder. But first you have to get hired.

The professions -- medicine, law, teaching, social
work, accounting, engineering and data processing --
became viable alternatives to small business as
increasing numbers of Jews went to college. Starting
at the time of the Depression, many Jews took civil
service jobs. Widespread unemployment at that time
led to the introduction of merit systems and the Jews
fared well. By the early Sixties, a substantial proportion of Jewish college graduates were civil
servants, and public employees' unions, most notably
the United Federation of Teaders, won substantial
wage increases.

The ultimate Jewish profession is that of
comedian:

> Although Jews constitute only 3%
> of the U.S. population, 80% of the
> nation's professional comedians are
> Jewish. Why such domination of
> American humor? New York City Psy-
> chologist Samuel Janus, who once did
> a yearlong stint as a stand-up comic,
> thinks that he has the answer:
> Jewish humor is born of depression
> and alienation from the general
> culture. For Jewish comedians, he
> told the recent annual meeting of
> the American Psychological Associ-
> ation, "comedy is a defense mecha-
> nism to ward off the aggression and
> hostility of others."[16]

This role is in perfect accord with Veblen's thesis
that the Jew is an outsider and a social critic.

Why are Jews different from all other Americans?
Nathaniel Weyl asserts that Jews are genetically

superior as a "result of a two-thousand-year process of selective breeding for intelligence."[17] He reasons that the brightest people during the Middle Ages were clergymen. While the Christians suffered genetically for not permitting their priests to reproduce, the rabbis were much sought-after as prospective husbands. Although plausible, the notion is unpleasantly reminiscent of Aryanism.

F. Jewish Political Power

According to Veblen's analysis, the Jews are not full-fledged members of society. Being outsiders, while not a chosen role, worked to their advantage. It would be wrong, of course, to equate American anti-Semitism with the forms it took in other countries. Not only are we a nation of immigrants, but the Jews are but one of many minorities. Only Protestants, or perhaps middle Americans make up a clear majority.

The Jewish population of the United States could hardly be called unified, except occasionally on a few volatile issues. While some Jews hold positions of considerable influence, there is very little evidence that they use their power to advance so-called Jewish interests. They will perhaps rally defensively when Israel is attacked or a case of home-grown anti-Semitism surfaces, but there is no conscious advancement of a Jewish cause. The indifference of Jews who have made it helps explain why other Jews have been unable to progress in large sectors of the economy. Had leverage been exerted at the proper places, undoubtedly more doors would have opened. Large commercial banks in New York, for example, not only have many Jewish customers and depositors, but even a few Jewish directors. Yet there is apparently no pressure to persuade banks to hire more Jewish executives.

The efforts of the large Jewish organizations, particularly the American Jewish Committee and B'nai B'rith, might best be described as reluctant, hesitant, and ineffectual. If these groups are not pushing, how can we expect the individual Jews in positions of influence to be breaking down employment barriers by themselves?

If the political power of Jews is even greater than their economic power, how have they used it to

19

open corporate doors? Not only has almost nothing
been done on this score, but ironically, Jewish political pressure has recently focused on political and
economic advancement of Blacks. Unfortunately, some
Jews -- as well as many other Americans -- now demur
that Blacks have gained too much, too fast.

In his very perceptive book, Jews and American
Politics, Stephen Isaacs observes that the role of
American Jews is comparable to that of the court Jews
in Europe: "Here one calls them strategists, computer
experts, media managers, fund raisers, but in the main
they are still raising money and doing chores for the
Protestants and Catholics who can hire the manpower
to fight their [political] wars."[18]

From the time of Mordechai in Persia to Kissinger
in the 1970's, Jews have characteristically assumed
this role. Jews not only provide technical expertise,
but a large part of the funds as well. Isaacs states
that more than half the large contributions to national
Demcratic campaigns come from Jews.[19] Ironically,
although 1972 marked the first large defection of
Jewish money and votes from the Democrats, Isaacs
noted that twelve of the twenty who made the White
House "enemy list" that year were Jews.[20]

Although the Jewish political record of the last
few decades is relatively honorable, the motives
haven't been entirely altruistic. According to Isaacs,
it is mostly fear that motivates the Jews to fight for
a "just" society, since only the existence of such a
society can ensure Jewish survival. Survival, of
course, is rather important to the Jews.

To return to our initial paradox -- that Jews
are wealthy but oppressed -- we see that Jews have
certainly prospered, but could have done even better.
To a certain extent, the fault is their own, because
they did not apply the necessary political and economic leverage to secure more than token representation in the corporate sector. The absence of such
pressure is understandable, however, in light of long-
standing Jewish attitudes. This too shall pass, so
don't make waves. American Jews are wealthy enough,
so why press their luck? Although unique to American
thinking, this is a normal attitude for any group
that has experienced long and brutal oppression.

Veblen's thesis that outsiders often prosper is
supported by the analogies we have noted of the

Indians and Pakistanis, overseas Chinese and Palestinians (as well as the Jews in many other countries).
It is impossible to substantiate our assertion that
the income of American Jews could have been greater.
We suspect, however, that it is at least possible that
employment discrimination has affected the level of
Jewish incomes.

G. The Civil Service: Last Refuge of the Jewish
    College Graduate

     Discrimination is not always reflected solely by
lower earnings. A particular group may be forced to
do unpleasant lower-status jobs with pay comparable to
our economy's more desirable jobs. The New York City
school teachers, nearly two-thirds of whom are
Jewish,[21] have recently won substantial pay increases,
putting them on a par with the lower rung of middle
management in private industry. Although the teachers'
hours are relatively short and vacations long, most
of their jobs consist of supervising unruly masses of
ghetto children, whom their keepers refer to as
"animals". Perhaps the most telling comment about
their status and self-image was that of a young female
teacher in a Brooklyn Junior High School: "I'd never
marry a teacher." Other civil service jobs are equally
demeaning. The welfare investigator and state employment interviewer do not generally deal with our
society's elite. Nor do the Jews who staff the myriad
bureaucracies of city, state, and federal government.
But what is most telling about these positions is the
status they provide.

     Consider, then, the alternatives open to Jewish
college graduates. Medical and law schools are both
becoming increasingly difficult to get into and pay
for. Graduate schools, which most people never finish,
provide degrees of questionable vocational value.
That leaves the corporations and the civil service.

     Corporations would appear to provide the more
attractive alternative. Although they require a
certain degree of conformity, this does not prove a
major drawback for most Jews, especially those who
have majored in business or accounting. The pay is
generally higher, and the financial prospects are
almost unlimited. The status of a corporate executive
is considerably higher than that of a federal venereal
disease investigator or welfare case worker.

21

Why, then, do so many Jews opt for the least attractive alternatives? If positions in the civil service are so desirable, why don't more WASP'S work there? Do the Jews have a monopoly? There can be only one answer to these questions: most large corporations discriminate against Jews.

The major obstacle to even greater Jewish prosperity and status is the anti-Semitic employment practices of large corporations. These have remained in effect while college, medical and law school quotas have been abolished, enabling Jews to earn high incomes. Society deems them as suitable professionals, but not corporate executives. Perhaps that would be a little too close.

Jews, like Blacks and women, are crowded out of corporate jobs. But since Jews are college graduates, they are able to secure other relatively well-paying positions. Although employment discrimination has not unduly affected Jewish incomes, it has had considerable effect on the type of jobs Jews obtain. They have been forced to seek jobs that require additional training beyond the Bachelor's degree (such as medicine or law), or they have fallen into low-status civil service jobs. In each case, the labor market has been distorted by employment discrimination.

Does our society prescribe certain economic roles for its various racial, religious, ethnic and sexual groups? If such a role can be discerned for the Jews, a relatively high-income group, then what are the roles reserved for those even lower in the economic pecking order? These indications of residual anti-Semitism have disturbing implications which we will be investigating further in Chapter IX.

Chapter Notes

1. Norval D. Glenn and Ruth Hyland, "Religious Preference and Worldly Success: Some Evidence from National Surveys," American Sociological Review, Vol. 35, February 1965.

2. Ibid.

3. Ibid.

4. According to a study conducted by Sidney Goldstein, of all the college graduates in the Providence area, a greater percentage of Jews than non-Jews went on to graduate or professional school. See Sidney Goldstein, The Greater Providence Jewish Community: A Population Survey. (Providence: The General Jewish Committee of Providence, 1964). This same point is made by Nathaniel Weyl. See The Jew in American Politics (New Rochelle, N.Y.: Arlington House, 1968), Chapter 13.

5. Any high school graduate from the New York City area applying to the better private colleges will testify to the fact that these quotas exist. Until the early 1950's there were overt quotas for Jewish applicants, but the current quotas have substantially the same effect.

   Benjamin Epstein and Arnold Forster published actual rejection letters from colleges. One, form Marjorie Webster Junior College, dated January 16, 1961, advised the applicant that "our quota of students of the Jewish faith has been filled." Another, dated July 29, 1959, found a more substantial reason for rejecting Jewish applicants: "Past experience has taught us that the Jewish girls find it difficult to fit into our schedules because of different times of church services and religious holidays." See Epstein and Forster, "Some of My Best Friends ..." (New York: Farrar, Straus and Cudahy, 1962), pp. 143 - 44.

6. Goldstein, op. cit. and Weyl, loc. cit.

7. Nathan Glazer and Daniel Moynihan, Beyond the Melting Pot (Cambridge, Mass.: The M.I.T. Press, 1970), 2nd Ed., p. 137.

8.   According to the Statistical Abstract of the
United States, 1975 (U.S. Bureau of the Census,
Washington, D.C., p. 123) someone 25 or older with
an eighth grade education has an average income of
$7,900 compared with an average of $16,600 for a 25-
year old college graduate. Also, see Paul C. Glick
and H.M. Miller, "Educational Level and Potential
Income," American Sociological Review, Vol. 21, June
1956.

9.   U.S. Bureau of the Census, op. cit., p. 393.

10. See, e.g., Galen L. Gockel, "Income and Religious
Affiliation," American Journal of Sociology, Vol. 74,
May 1969.

11. See Gockel, op. cit., Goldstein, op. cit., and
Donald J. Bogue, The Population of the United States
(New York: Free Press, 1959).

12. Nearly all of this section appeared in the Jewish
Spectator, Summer, 1979.

13. Thorstein Veblen, "The Intellectual Pre-eminence
of Jews in Modern Europe," Political Science Quarterly,
March 1919.

14. Harry Golden, The Greatest Jewish City in the
World (Garden City, N.Y.: Doubleday, 1972), p. 76.

15. Leo Rosten, Hollywood: The Movie Colony; the
Movie Makers (New York: Harcourt Brace, 1941), p. 67.

16. Time Magazine, "Analyzing Jewis Comics: It's
just that it hurts less when you laugh," October 2,
1978, p. 76.

17. Weyl, op. cit., p. 10.

18. Stephen Isaacs, Jews and American Politics
(Garden City, N.Y.: Doubleday, 1974), p. 13.

19. Isaacs, op. cit., p. 6.

20. Isaacs, op. cit., pp. 8 - 9.

21. See Harry Golden, op. cit., p. 99. Golden also
notes that 80% of New York's social workers are
Jewish (p. 6).

CHAPTER III

DISCRIMINATION IN SELECTED INDUSTRIES:
THE EARLIER EVIDENCE[1]

> Jews are a complementary nation;
> when they become competitive they
> are expelled by the host nation.
> > Feliks Gross, Professor
> > Emeritus of Sociology,
> > Brooklyn College

A. Introduction

Most Americans would acknowledge that there are
traditional black jobs and white jobs. Women's work
includes nursing and typing; while medicine and
management are masculine preserves. During recent
years, both Blacks and women have lodged forceful
protests against the blatant job discrimination they
have always experienced. Job allocation on the basis
of race and sex can easily be observed. All you have
to do is look.

Anti-Semitic hiring practices are not only harder to observe, but are not even acknowledged by most Jews, let alone by the rest of the population. Most people believe that this type of discrimination has all but disappeared since World War II. Recently, however, protest among other white ethnic groups has begun to surface. The so-called hyphenated Americans, most notably the Italian-Americans, have even been holding rallies to display their indignation at being stereotyped.

No one would maintain that Jews are more offended against than these other groups. The experience of Blacks as well as that of women have been brutal. Americans of East- and South-European origin have also been victims of considerable prejudice regardless of their religion. America remains a bigoted society: equality of opportunity is about as realistic a description of conditions here as were the stories about all that gold in the streets.

In this chapter we will look at some of the evidence of employment discrimination against Jews, particularly Jewish college graduates. We will examine, in turn, employment practices in banking, insurance, the automobile industry, the oil industry and the large public utilities. These data, gathered largely in the Fifties and Sixties, will provide a historical background for our own study, which begins in the next chapter. Until quite recently, Jews had considerable difficulty finding jobs in any of these industries.

B. Banking

> You may have a friend at Chase
> Manhattan, but do you have a
> relative?

The existence of an international Jewish bankers' communist conspiracy was a widely accepted belief in the Thirties.[2] Those who were receptive toward this unfortunate view of Jews were rarely troubled by reconciling the obvious conflict between banking and communism. The subtler unlikelihood, however, was being Jewish and being a banker. Perhaps the myth of Jewish pre-eminence in finance is bolstered by lingering visions of medieval moneylenders.

Do many Jews work in banks today? If Jews once
were underrepresented in banking, has their lot
improved considerably since World War II? Several
surveys conducted since then have indicated that no
more than one per cent of all bank executives are
Jewish.

In 1960, an American Jewish Committee (AJC)
study of six leading commercial banks in Philadelphia
disclosed that only 12 of 1216 executives were
Jewish.[3] Five later surveys turned up very similar
results (see Tables I - V below). Such findings,
which could undermine the myth of Jewish pre-
eminence in banking, have not been sufficiently
publicized.

Even the 1966 figures somewhat overstate the
importance of Jews in banking. These eight senior
executives in Table II represented five banks while
the other 45 banks had no Jewish senior executives.
Similarly, only 32 out of more than 3400 junior
executives were Jewish. Again the few Jews were
concentrated in 12 of the 50 banks, and the others
had no Jewish junior executives.

Data on commercial banks in New York City, also
in 1966 (shown in Table III), are even more revealing.
Even in New York City, Jews were not found to be
more heavily represented in banking than they were
in the rest of the country. Here, in the "greatest
Jewish city in the world" (where half the college
graduates are Jewish), the banks were able to find
only ten qualified Jews -- a bare minyan!

In 1973 the AJC looked at the management of
the country's 15 largest commercial banks, 8 of
which are in New York City. They found not one
Jew among the 176 senior executives. These results
can easily be verified in any financial library.
The 15 leading commercial banks were listed in the
July 1974 issue of Fortune, while the names of the
officers of each can be found in Standard and Poor's
Register of Corporations, Directors and Executives.

Jews constitute at least five per cent of the
college graduates in the metropolitan areas of each
of the cities listed in Table V. In Chicago, Detroit,
and Pittsburgh, where over ten per cent of the college

TABLE I

Employment of Jews in Nine Leading Commercial Banks
in the District of Columbia -- 1966*

	Total Number	Number of Jews	Jews as a % of Total
Senior Executives	152	1	0.7%
Middle Management	281	2	0.7%
Total Executives	433	3	0.7%

* Survey conducted by Wayne State University for the
U.S. Equal Employment Opportunity Commission.

Source: The American Jewish Committee, Patterns of
Exclusion from the Executive Suite: Commercial Banking
(New York: American Jewish Committee, 1967) (mimeo),
p. 5.

TABLE II

Employment of Jews in the 50 Leading Commercial Banks
in the U.S. -- 1966

	Total Number	Number of Jews	Jews as a % of Total
Senior Executives	632	8	1.3%
Junior Executives	3438	32	0.9%
Total Executives	4070	40	1.0%

Source: The American Jewish Committee, Patterns of
Exclusion from the Executive Suite: Commercial Banking
(New York: American Jewish Committee , 1967) (mimeo),
pp. 3 - 4.

TABLE III

Employment of Jews in the Nine Leading Commercial Banks
in New York City -- 1966

	Total Number	Number of Jews	Jews as a % of Total
Senior Executives	173	1	0.6%
Junior Executives	927	9	1.0%
Total	1100	10	0.9%

Source: See Table II

TABLE IV

Employment of Jews in Middle and Senior Management
in the 15 Largest Commercial Banks -- 1973

	Total Number	Number of Jews	Jews as a % of Total
Senior Management	176	0	0%
Middle Management	1757	14	0.8%
Total	1933	14	0.7%

Source: The American Jewish Committee, Summary of
Reports on First Fifteen Banks (New York: American
Jewish Committee, 1973) (Report # 73 - 610 - 29)
(mimeo).

TABLE V

Employment of Jews in Middle and Senior Management
in 21 Leading Commercial Banks -- 1973

Bank and City	Senior Management		Junior Management	
	Total	Jewish	Total	Jewish
First National Bank of Boston	22	0	263	2
First National Bank of Chicago	13	0	303	10
Central National Bank of Cleveland	11	0	71	2
Cleveland Trust Company	10	0	60	3
National City Bank of Cleveland	5	0	67	0
Cleveland Total	26	0	198	5
First National Bank in Dallas	36	1	121	1
Republic National Bank -- Dallas	25	0	126	1
Dallas Total	61	1	247	2
Detroit Bank and Trust Company	13	0	79	0
Manufacturers National Bank of Detroit	9	0	126	2
National Bank of Detroit	10	0	178	1
Detroit Total	32	0	383	3

TABLE V -- Continued

Bank and City	Senior Management		Junior Management	
	Total	Jewish	Total	Jewish
First City National Bank of Houston	19	0	111	0
Texas Commerce Bank -- Houston	24	0	90	1
Houston Total	43	0	191	1
Fidelity Bank -- Philadelphia	14	0	73	2
Girard Trust Bank	15	0	77	0
Philadelphia National Bank	20	0	78	3
Philadelphia Total	49	0	228	5
Mellon National Bank	12	0	146	0
Pittsburgh National Bank	10	0	133	1
Pittsburgh Total	22	0	279	1
First National Bank of Oregon	14	0	150	0
United States National Bank of Oregon	11	0	114	0
Portland Total	25	0	264	0
National Bank of Commerce of Seattle	10	0	50	0
Seattle -- First National Bank	4	0	156	1
Total Seattle	14	0	206	1

Source: See Table IV.

graduate population is Jewish, not one of the 67
senior bank executives was Jewish, while only 14 of
the 965 junior executives were Jewish. Among these
banks, Mellon National did not have one Jew among its
158 officers, nor were there any Jews among Detroit
National's 92 officers.

The record is no different in Cleveland and
Philadelphia, where approximately one college graduate
in five is Jewish. Once again, none of the 75 senior
officers and only 10 of the 426 junior executives at
the six surveyed banks were Jews. Even though these
cities have substantial numbers of Jewish college
graduates, there were none among Central Bank of
Cleveland's 72 officers, nor among the 92 at Girard
Trust Company.

Finally we have the case of First National Bank
of Boston, which is located in an area where over one-
third of the college graduates are Jews. From this
vast pool of talent, which includes thousands of
graduates from prestigious colleges and business
schools, this bank could come up with just two Jewish
officers, both of whom were on the junior management
level. First National Bank of Boston is just one
instance of a pattern of underrepresentation of Jews
among the ranks of banking executives. In none of the
21 banks surveyed were the number of Jewish executives
even remotely proportionate to their percentage share
of the local college graduate population.

According to the American Jewish Committee's
analysis of their data on banking:

> The New York findings may be
> described as particularly extreme
> because banks -- unlike many other
> large business organizations --
> employ most of their personnel in a
> single locality, or, at most, in one
> state, and thus may reasonably be
> expected to reflect local ethnic
> configurations in their staffs. In
> New York City, exclusive of suburbs,
> Jews make up nearly one-quarter of
> the population and about half of the
> college graduates.[4]

The employment policies of New York's leading commercial banks have led to these lopsided results: less than one per cent of the officers are drawn from half the college graduate population of New York, while the remaining 99 per cent are drawn from the other half. Perhaps it would be possible to attribute this unusual pattern to chance factors if it occurred at just one bank. However, the absence of Jewish officers is a pattern in each of New York's nine leading commercial banks.

Apparently exclusion of Jews from management is not confined to commercial banks. In another AJC survey, it was found that 41 of 50 of New York City's mutual savings banks had no key officers who were Jewish. Among more than 400 officers, only 9 were Jews.[5]

Furthermore, a 1967 AJC report noted that "some 12 to 15% of the living graduates of the Harvard Business School are Jews, [but] fewer than one per cent of the young men who go from Harvard Business School into commercial banking are Jews."[6] Once again we might ask -- are they avoiding us, or are we avoiding them?

But the Jewish banking conspiracy theory still won't die. After a speech at Duke University Law School on October 10, 1974, General George S. Brown, chairman of the Joint Chief of Staff, made one of the most celebrated anti-Semitic remarks of all time. According to the New York Times, General Brown observed that the Jewish influence is "so strong, you wouldn't believe it, now. They own, you know, the banks in the country, the newspapers. Just look at where the Jewish money is."[7]

The inaccuracy of General Brown's statement almost rivals its offensiveness. Senator William Proxmire (Wisconsin Democrat), now Chairman of the Senate Banking Committee, noted that "probably no industry in the country has more consistently and cruelly rejected Jews from positions of power and influence than commercial banking."[8]

The huge influx of foreign exchange into the oil-producing Arab countries has also had some anti-Semitic repercussions in the banking field. The widely-publicized blacklisting of Jewish banks (all of which, incidentally, are European) has given the false impression that there are substantial Jewish banking interests in the United States. Perhaps more to the point, an article in New York's Village Voice raised the question, "Is a WASP bank going to be quite so keen as it might have been to hire young people who might offend Arab clients, or clients doing business with the Arabs?"[9]

In a recent book on bankers, Martin Mayer suggested that Arabs might actually be trying to avoid New York, rather than New York banks: "Not that they would have to do business with Jews at the New York banks, of course; but they couldn't easily avoid Jewish cabbies and shoe salesmen and real estate agents."[10]

General Brown's view notwithstanding, Jews are virtually unrepresented among bank executives, both in New York and throughout the nation. Undoubtedly the misconception exists in the minds of many Americans. Whether the Arab economic boycott will affect Jewish employment in banking is a moot point, given the small number of Jewish executives currently in banking. We will be discussing this topic in much greater detail in Chapter VIII.

C. Insurance

Insurance is another industry supposedly run by Jews. We shall see that although there are a substantial number of Jewish people employed by insurance companies, they are hardly running the industry. Invariably, Jews are shunted away from the home office, where the major decisions are made, out into sales. This was reflected in the results of the 1959 Anti-Defamation League (ADL) study shown in Tables VI and VII.

Even in the New York are, less than six per cent of the insurance executives were Jewish. While 66 of the 658 sales executives, or 10%, were Jewish, only 77 of the 1733 home office executives, or 4% were Jewish. This is hardly a picture of Jewish dominance. In another ADL analysis of the employment of Jews in insurance companies outside New York, this pattern was borne out. The 73 Jewish executives in home offices (listed in Table VII) comprised less than four per cent of the total. Furthermore, 48, or two-thirds

TABLE VI

Employment of Jews in Five Insurance Companies in the
Greater New York Area -- 1959

	Total Employment	Number of Jews	Jews as a % of Total
Home Office	1733	71	4.1%
Sales	658	66	10.0%
Total	2393	137	5.7.

Source: Anti-Defamation League, Rights, Vol. 7,
No. 1, June 1968, p. 123.

TABLE VII

Employment of Jews in Seven Insurance Companies Outside
New York -- 1959

	Total Employment	Number of Jews	Jews as a % of Total
Home Office	2020	73	3.6%
Sales and Branch Offices	4046	251	6.2%
Total	6066	324	5.3%

Source: See Table VI.

of them held jobs requiring a specific skill --
actuary, accountant, physician, or attorney. These
are staff jobs, and not part of the decision-making
management apparatus.

The dichotomy between home office and sales is
particularly significant. The position reserved for
Jews is symbolic of their role in our economy -- they
are relegated to the periphery rather than the center
of operations. And even at the center, they tend to
be technicians and professionals, not "real" management.

In a more recent ADL survey of 10 Hartford-based
insurance companies, only four of 367 officers and
directors were Jewish.[11] (We will note parenthetically
that Jews make up more than ten per cent of the population in the Hartford area and more than twenty per
cent of the area's college graduates.) The pattern
of exclusion of Jews from management is clear, both
in New York and on a national basis. Perhaps the
fact that Jews are the most heavily insured group
in the country has facilitated Jewish inroads into
insurance sales. However, the administrative apparatus
of insurance remains quite safe from Jewish dominance.

D. Automobiles

In the auto industry America has come a long way
since the Model T , but a close examination of the
128 top officers of the Big Three (listed in Standard
and Poor's Register of Corporations, Directors and
Executives, 1981) does not reveal a single Jewish
name. The auto industry has never seemed anxious
to put Jews in the driver's seat; the Anti-Defamation
League called it "Detroit's Old Habit" in the ADL
Bulletin, Nov., 1963.

Table VII pretty much tells the story of the
absence of Jews in the auto industry. Even this tiny
percentage overstates the management role of Jews,
since many of these high level employees are

TABLE VIII

Employment of Jews in White Collar, Professional, and
  Executive Jobs in the Automobile Industry -- 1963

Company	Number of Jews Employed
Ford	146
Chrysler	102
General Motors	79
Total	327

Source: Anti-Defamation League. "Detroit's Old
Habit," The ADL Bulletin, Vol. 20, No. 9, November
1963, pp. 1 - 2.

technicians, engineers, and scientists. For example,
20 of the 146 Jews at Ford are in the Scientific
Research Laboratory, while 17 of the 102 at Chrysler
are in the Missile Division.

These 327 Jews represent less than one per cent
of the 51,000 white collar, professional and executive
personnel employed by the automobile industry in 1963.
If we keep in mind that over ten per cent of the
college graduates living in the Detroit area are
Jewish, it is apparent that Jews are very underrepresented in this industry. Many prominent members of
Detroit's Jewish community readily acknowledge that
they are not sought out by the auto firms. A wealthy
Jewish retailer in Detroit put it, "The Jews know
where they're not wanted." This point is illustrated
quite literally by the residential pattern of the
five municipalities of Grosse Pointe, where many auto
executives reside. Jews, as well as other minorities,
have been virtually excluded from this area.

The Big Three employ very few, if any, Jews,
in the sales and finance divisions. There are even
[ADL] documented reports of the car and truck
manufacturers refusing to deal with Jewish personnel
in advertising. A Jewish account executive is about
as welcome in Detroit as in Saudi Arabia.

E. Oil

Closely allied with the auto industry are the
large oil companies. Of the ten leading industrial
corporations listed by Fortune by size of sales in
1981, five are oil companies[12] and three of the others
are General Motors, Ford, and Chrysler. Since
gasoline is their main product, it is not surprising
that oil lobbyists find themselves in agreement with
the auto lobby on high trust funds, pollution-
control devices, and oil-depletion allowances.
Furthermore, any contention that Jews occupy positions
of major importance in our economy can be refuted
on the basis of their exclusion from both the oil and
auto industries.

Anti-Semitic employment practices in the oil
industry are fairly common knowledge. On the basis
of AJC data, between one and four per cent of all oil
industry executives are Jewish.[13] Of course, this

may not be due entirely to discriminatory hiring practices, since Jews are also disinclined to apply.

An Anti-Defamation League study published in 1978 found only five Jews among the top 300 executives at the six leading oil companies -- Mobil, Exxon, Texaco, Standard Oil of California, Gulf, and Shell.[14] The virtual absence of Jews, according to the study, was due mainly to classic discrimination including, "recruitment avoidance, promotion levels beyond which Jews cannot go, non-assignment of Jews to certain job areas, and stereotyped employment (i.e., in such departments as legal, accounting, and research)."[15]

In a 1971 civil suit against Standard Oil of California, Monroe Baer, Jr., who had been an attorney with the company for 19 years, charged that he had been discriminated against because he was Jewish. According to a New York Times account, Baer charged that his religion was the reason he had been eliminated from consideration for promotion to a position in Washington, D.C.

> He said that "somebody asked, 'Mr. Baer isn't Jewish, is he?' And they were told 'as a matter of fact he is' and they said, 'that'll eliminate him from consideration then.'"

> He was told, he said, that as a Jew he could not become a member of some important Washington clubs, which would limit his effectiveness, and that the Arab nations from which the company buys petroleum might be offended at dealing with a Jew.

> His big trouble came, he said, after he hired first one, then a second Jewish lawyer to work on his six-man legal staff. He was called before a vice president and told he was to be removed from his job and downgraded.[16]

The case dragged on for several years until finally Baer agreed to settle for several hundred thousand dollars in damages. The key condition of the settlement was that Baer never discuss his case.

F. Public Utilities

In 1963 quite a flap was created when the findings of an AJC study was published on the front page of the New York Times.[17] Less than one per cent of all public utility executives were found to be Jewish. The companies included A.T. & T., Western Union, Con Edison, as well as 47 other gas and electric companies. Out of 755 officers, these companies had just eight Jewish officers.

That was in 1963. Eight years later, another AJC survey found virtually no change in Jewish employment in the public utility field. This time, however, the results were kept confidential,[18] probably to avoid the wrath of the Jewish establishment, not to mention that of the public utility companies themselves.

Of the top 50 public utilities in 1971, there were 17 Jews among the 942 officers. However, ten of these had recently been hired by Con Edison upon the accession of Charles Luce. Of the remaining 49 utilities, one had two Jewish officers, five had one Jew each, and 43 had no Jewish executives.

G. The Clubs

Jews and other minority group members have long been denied membership in many of the nation's exclusive "downtown" clubs and country clubs. Since a great deal of business is conducted at these clubs -- whether over dinner, in the steam room, or on the golf course -- those who are denied membership cannot deal on an equal footing with their colleagues. Corporations often pay the dues of their executives, which are considered a business expense.

One instance vividly depicts the importance of membership in such clubs:

40

In the late 1950s, now-deceased
Edward Gudeman, who had been "groomed
for the top job" at Sears, Roebuck &
Co., Chicago, was reportedly passed
over when that position finally opened.
The explanation: He was told that as
a Jew he wouldn't be admitted to the
exclusive Chicago clubs where other
executives meet....[19]

In 1969 an American Jewish Committee survey
revealed that "Out of some 1,800 downtown men's clubs,
roughly 80% have no Jewish members....Still, this
represents some change from the 90% exclusion rate
10 years ago...."[20]

A minor uproar was touched off in 1976 when two
of Jimmy Carter's prospective Cabinet appointees --
Griffin Bell (Attorney General) and Bert Lance
(Budget Director) -- were found to be members of
Atlanta clubs that barred Jews and blacks. The New
York Times reported that "Jim Custance, manager of the
Piedmont Club which is similar in tradition to the
Capital City Club as a center for high society in
Atlanta, said he knew of no blacks or Jews among the
1,000 members.[21]

But more to the point, these two clubs are not
exceptions, but rather still the rule:

The most frequently heard
complaint in Atlanta today is:
Why us? "There are thousands of
clubs all over the country that
have been restricted against Jews
and blacks and Orientals and what
have you for years!" says one in-
dignant woman. "Why is everyone
picking on poor little Atlanta?"[22]

Nassau County on Long Island is about 50% Jewish.
But some of the clubs on the Island don't always

reflect these figures. A recent New York Times article describes one such club:

> A white, Anglo-Saxon Protestant insurance executive who says he "fit in like wallpaper" at exclusive Long Island country clubs for 20 years sued the North Hempstead Country Club today, claiming that it had cancelled his membership when he tried to change club rules to admit blacks, Jews and people from other minority groups.

The article goes on to state that

> Officers of the country club were unavailable for comment yesterday, but its president, Charles Hyde Walker, has been quoted in Newsday, the Long Island newspaper, as saying that blacks "would probably not survive the admissions process" and that the few Jewish families admitted to the club "probably got in because they did not allude to the fact of their Jewishness, and we don't run F.B.I.-type background investigations here."

If Jews (and blacks and women) are still denied membership in the very clubs that cater to the nation's top-ranking corporate executives, then how welcome are they in the corporate executive suites? You've got the same guys at the door deciding who gets in and who doesn't.

In a major study put together by the American Jewish Committee, it was found that while substantial progress had been made over the last decade, scores of country clubs throughout America still barred not only Jews, but blacks and women as well. For example, in New Jersey, the Echo Lake Country Club (Westfield) is "Closed to Jewish and Black membership," as are the Essex County Country Club, the Forest Hills Club (Bloomfield), Glen Ridge Country Club, Rock Spring

42

ountry Club (West Orange), Short Hills Club,
lopatcong Yacht Club, West Orange Women's Club,
rcola Country Club (Paramus), Knickerbocker Country
lub (Tenafly), Ridgewood Country Club, Englewood
len's Club, Deal Golf & Country Club, Sea View Country
lub (Absecon), and the Trenton Country Club.[24] In
Jew York, the Apawanis, Mt. Kisco Country Club, Pelham
lanor, Siwanoy, St. Andrews, Westchester Hills, Winged
'oot, and Wykagyl are all "restricted."[25]

The problem is evidently much worse in the suburbs
than in the major cities. In New York, for example,
according to Burt Siegel, Director of the American
Jewish Committee's Executive Suite Program, the Links
and the Union Club, long two gentile strongholds of
lanhattan, are now admitting a few affluent Jews.

In an internally distributed memorandum, Israel
aster, then Director of the American Jewish Com-
littee's Executive Suite Program recommended:

> A corporation should consider not
> paying dues for their exclusive clubs
> which discriminate on the basis of
> religion, race or ethnic background
> and should avoid attending meetings
> held at such clubs. The Bank of
> America and an increasing number
> of large corporations have adopted
> this approach or policy.[26]

4. Conclusion

Contrary to "common knowledge," Jews are still
excluded from banks, insurance companies, oil companies, etc. Perhaps the most succinct description of
the role of the Jew in the American economy is found
in an article by Aviva Cantor Zuckoff:

> Till today, Jews have not been
> and are not really involved in the
> production process but are predominant
> in the distribution end of the economy.

> The thin spreading of token Jews in
> such institutions as banks, utilities,
> large corporations, the diplomatic
> service and government only serves
> to illustrate the exclusion of the
> Jews from them.

> Jews have always been allowed and
> even encouraged however, to enter
> new areas of the economy that were
> too risky for anyone else. Jews were
> essential in the incipient states of
> capitalism; the rising goyish bourgeoi-
> sie took it over when it became too
> profitable.[27]

The industrial and financial sectors are the muscula-
ture and central nervous system of our economy, yet
the Jews who are almost entirely absent from these
sectors are supposedly running things.

How is the Jew's peripheral economic role
reflected in his characteristic career path? Until
the late Forties, entree to the executive suite was
usually gained by working one's way up from a clerical
position. By the mid-Fifties, however, the majority
of corporate executives were obtaining their first
management positions upon graduation from college.
Nearly all the large corporations, banks, insurance
companies, and public utilities send representatives
to colleges to recruit employees with executive
potential. The recruiting and initial hiring policies
are obviously crucial to those aspiring to corporate
management. The rest of this book will analyze
corporate recruiting patterns and their implications
with respect to Jewish college graduates. Data from
college placement offices, executive search agencies
and college alumni associations will be examined along
with information from corporations themselves and from
public records.

44

Chapter Notes

1. Most of this chapter appeared in Jewish Currents, February, 1978.

2. See, for example, Chapter 12 of Arnold Forster and Benjamin Epstein, The New Anti-Semitism (New York: McGraw-Hill, 1974).

3. See The American Jewish Committee, Patterns of Exclusion from the Executive Suite : Commercial Banking (New York: American Jewish Committee, 1967) (mimeo), p. 5.

4. American Jewish Committee, op. cit., pp. 4 - 5.

5. AJC. The Mutual Savings Banks of New York City (New York: AJC, 1965), p. 1.

6. AJC, Patterns of Exclusion from the Executive Suite: Commercial Banking (New York: AJC, 1967), p. 10.

7. John W. Finney, "Chairman of Joint Chiefs Regrets Remarks on Jews," New York Times, November 14, 1974, p. 1.

8. Associated Press story appearing in the New York Post, November 14, 1974, p. 5.

9. Alexander Cockburn and James Ridgeway, "The Arab Blacklist and the Jewish Banks," The Village Voice, February 24, 1975.

10. Martin Mayer, The Bankers (New York: Weybright and Talley, 1974), p. 478.

11. Anti-Defamation League, Rights, Vol. 7, No. 1, June 1968, p. 123.

12. Fortune, May 1981. The five leading oil companies are Exxon, Texaco, Mobil, Gulf, and Standard Oil of California.

13. Confidential minutes of meeting between representatives of oil companies and the AJC.

14.   Ira Gissen, ed., "A Study of Jewish Employment Problems in the Big Six Oil Company Headquarters," Rights, Summer, 1978, Vol. 9, No. 1, p. 5.

15.   Gissen, op. cit., p. 3.

16.   Wallace Turner, "Oil Company Sued On Charge Of Bias," The New York Times, April 20, 1972, p. 32.

17.   New York Times, December 29, 1963, p. 1.

18.   AJC, Discrimination in the Public Utilities Industry -- 8 Years After (Draft #2) (Mimeo), August 12, 1971.

19.   Industry Week, "What's Happening at the Club," August 4, 1980, p. 43.

20.   Elliot Carlson, "Civil Rights and Clubs," The Wall Street Journal, September 10, 1969.

21.   Paul Delaney, "Discrimination Remains a Policy and a Practice at Many Clubs," The New York Times, September 13, 1976, p. 29.

22.   Stephen Birmingham, "The clubs Griffin Bell had to quit," The New York Times Magazine, February 6, 1977, p. 70.

23.   New York Times, "White Protestant Sues Club On L.I. Over Minority Bias," November 14, 1979, page B2.

24.   The American Jewish Committee, Social Club Discrimination Survey 1979 - 1968 (mimeo) (New York: American Jewish Committee, 1980), pp. 6 - 9.

25.   Ibid., pp. 9 - 10.

26.   Israel Laster, Overcoming Barriers to Executive Careers (mimeo) (New York: American Jewish Committee, September, 1978), p. 15.

27.   Aviva Cantor Zuckoff, "The Oppression of America's Jews," in Jack Nusan Porter and Peter Drier, eds., Jewish Radicalism (New York: Grove Press, 1973), p. 30.

CHAPTER IV. CORPORATE RECRUITMENT PATTERNS[1]

A. Introduction

There are apparently very few Jewish executives
employed by large American corporations such as banks,
insurance companies and public utilities. Although
the situation is believed to have improved over the
last two decades, the data shown in this Chapter will
not support this view.

Any disappearance of hiring practices that seem
to be shunning Jews, should be reflected in corporate
recruitment patterns. If Jewish executives are now
being hired in proportion to their numbers in the
college graduate population -- about 10 per cent --
then one would expect to see a substantial number of
corporations sending recruiters to campuses with large
percentages of Jewish students. In fact, however,
few of America's large corporations ever send representatives to any college where Jews constitute at
least 30 per cent of the undergraduate student body.

Most college graduates hired by large corporations

47

are initially contacted by recruiters sent to their campuses. In this chapter, we will show that recruiters are apparently avoiding schools with large Jewish enrollments.

We will be looking at the corporate recruiting effort at some 170 colleges. They include private, public, large and small colleges around the country. Because the key variable was percentage of Jewish undergraduate enrollment, the schools selected ran from almost no Jews (Hardin-Simmons in Texas) to New York's Yeshiva University (98 per cent Jewish).[2]

Letters were sent to the placement directors of these schools, asking for lists of corporate recruiters who had visited the campus during the last academic year. As a cross-check, similar letters were sent to directors of college recruitment of some 800 corporations. To obtain Jewish enrollment figures, we wrote to college registrars and Hillel directors. It was now possible to match the placement data with the religious data.

The placement data obtained were based on the academic years 1972-73 or 1973-74. Neither were considered recession years although there was, of course, a considerable fall-off in campus recruitment in 1974-75. Of the 170 colleges surveyed, 128 provided usable data.

We have limited our survey of corporate recruiters to large industrial companies, banks, insurance companies and public utilities. As we noted in the previous chapter, these firms, rather than retail stores, intermediate-sized industrial firms, and various government agencies, are less likely to recruit and hire Jewish applicants.

We observed the behavior of two key variables -- Jewish enrollment and the number of campus visits by corporate recruiters. To examine what happens to the number of campus visits when Jewish enrollment rises, we divided the schools into four groups -- less than 10% Jewish enrollment, 10 - 19.9% Jewish, 20 - 29.9%, 30 - 39.9%, and 40% Jewish and over.

We have posed just one question here: Are campuses with high proportions of Jewish students as likely to be visited by corporate representatives as those with much lower Jewish enrollments?

B. The Data

Most of the college graduates recently hired by
large companies were recruited at campus interviews,
so the number of campus visits by corporate representatives may be taken as the basic measure of corporate hiring patterns. For each group of schools
(under 10 per cent Jewish to 40 per cent Jewish or
over) we calculated the average number of corporate
visits. For example, there were 19 schools with
Jewish enrollments between 10 per cent and 19.9 per
cent, which were visited by 183 insurance companies
and 108 banks (see Table I).

By comparing the average number of visits by
corporate recruiters from insurance companies, banks,
large industrial corporations and public utilities,
we can see how these averages vary with Jewish enrollments. When the Jewish enrollment goes beyond,
say, 30 per cent, if the average number of corporate
visits declines, this could mean that the corporations are avoiding these schools because of their
high Jewish enrollments, and if that decline is very
sharp, then this tendency would be quite clear.

Table I is more or less a summary table, showing
the average number of visits made by large industrial
corporations, insurance companies, banks and public
utilities to various colleges. Before analyzing this
data, let's explain each of the categories used here.
Fortune annually publishes a list of the nation's
top industrial firms ranked by sales. Leading the
list are such household names as General Motors,
Exxon, Ford, Chrysler, and General Electric. We've
followed the convention of separating this list into
the top 100 and the next 400 firms.

Banks, insurance companies and public utilities
are also ranked by Fortune. However, we have included
all banks including savings banks , mutual savings
banks, and savings and loan associations, because
commercial banks do only a limited amount of recruiting. Similarly, we have included all insurance
companies, rather than just the top 50.

Public utilities have been separated into the
top 50 and "Other Public Utilities." Because the
top 50 have been accused of being anti-Semitic, this
breakdown lends itself to an examination of this

49

TABLE I

AVERAGE NUMBER OF VISITS BY CORPORATIONS TO CAMPUSES
WITH VARYING JEWISH ENROLLMENTS
1972-1974

% of Undergraduate Enrollment that is Jewish	"Fortune's" top industrial firms		Insurance Companies	Banks	"Fortune's" top 50 Public Utilities	Other Public Utilities
	top 100	next 400				
Under 10	20.0	19.8	10.5	6.8	1.9	1.9
10 - 19.9	21.9	22.2	9.6	5.7	3.5	2.3
20 - 29.9	19.0	15.8	7.8	9.3	2.1	.9
30 - 39.9	13.6	9.2	8.6	5.2	1.2	.4
40 & over	4.3	3.5	7.5	3.5	.4	.1

charge. In our survey of the earlier evidence of employment discrimination (Chapter III), we noted that not only public utilities, but banks and insurance companies have few Jews in their executive ranks. These large firms have presumably mended their ways in recent years, but, as we turn to Table I, this change is not reflected in corporate recruitment figures.

Our classification of schools by Jewish enrollment lends itself to the detection of a "tipping point" at which corporations perceive the schools to be largely Jewish.[3] Not only are schools like Yeshiva (98% Jewish) or Brandeis (60% Jewish) bypassed by corporate recruiters but also Columbia (32.5%), Boston University (38.1%) and City College (31.3%). This tipping point apparently occurs somewhere between a 30 or 35% Jewish enrollment. The average number of recruiting visits by each type of company declines sharply at this point.

C. Analysis of the Data

The consistency of these figures seems particularly striking. With the exception of insurance companies, the average number of visits to schools with low Jewish enrollments (below 30 per cent) is higher than the number of visits made to schools with high Jewish enrollments. The average number of visits to colleges with Jewish enrollments in excess of 40 per cent, again with the exception of insurance companies, usually amounts to a third or a quarter of the visits to schools with low Jewish enrollment.

The data of Table I can be further refined. For one thing, we haven't allowed for size of school enrollment. Large and small colleges are considered together. One would expect, all other things being equal, for a corporate recruiter to prefer visiting larger rather than smaller schools. To interview a given number of students, he would have to do that much less travelling.

Because of the small number of colleges with high Jewish enrollments (now to be divided into three groups), we have combined the colleges with 30 - 39.9 per cent Jewish enrollments with those of 40 per cent or more.

Table IIA easily shows a repetition of the pattern established in Table I -- a sharp decline in all categories except insurance companies. While the industry is not averse to hiring Jewish salesmen, the welcome has not been extended to those who want to work on the "inside" (i.e., line management).[4] The results shown in Tables I and IIA are entirely consistent with our earlier analysis. With regard to industrial firms , banks, and public utilities, the decline at the 30 per cent Jewish enrollment mark is about 50 per cent in all five categories.

We have approximately the same results in Table IIB, except that here even insurance companies show a decline beyond the 30 per cent tipping point. In Table IIC there are much sharper declines beyond the 30 per cent tipping point, with the exception of insurance companies.

Since the schools with high Jewish enrollments among the larger schools include several colleges within the City University of New York (CUNY), one should not be surprised by the precipitous fall in recruiting by the large industrial companies and the banks. Although New York is the headquarters for hundreds of large industrial corporations, banks and insurance companies, only a handful send their recruiters to the colleges in the City University. Graduates can, of course, send their resumes or walk in off the street for an interview. However, according to many personnel officers and recruitment directors, the chances of such people being hired is usually infinitesimal.

We eventually located and interviewed a handful of City University graduates employed in large New York-based corporations. Oddly, each one seemed quite literally an "isolated case." Each knew of only a few other Jews among his colleagues, and of those a still smaller minority were City University graduates. This situation contrasts sharply with the usual preponderance of local graduates employed by large corporations based outside New York. Since the City University graduating classes have traditionally been close to two-thirds Jewish, it appears likely that the New York firms must have gone far out of their way in their recruitment visits.

Mr. Leonard Langer, the Recruitment Officer for Morgan Guaranty Trust Company, provided us with an almost amusing exchange which inadvertently

52

TABLE IIA

AVERAGE NUMBER OF VISITS OF CORPORATE RECRUITERS TO SCHOOLS
WITH ENROLLMENTS UNDER 5,000, WITH
VARYING JEWISH ENROLLMENTS
1972 – 1974

% of Undergraduate Enrollment that is Jewish	"Fortune's" top industrial firms		Insurance Companies	Banks	"Fortune's" top 50 Public Utilities	Other Public Utilities
	top 100	next 400				
Under 10	8.9	7.7	7.6	5.7	.8	.7
10 - 19.9	6.4	6.8	7.6	5.8	1.9	1.4
20 - 29.9	14.7	10.4	6.3	10.0	1.4	1.0
30 & over	7.4	4.7	6.8	4.4	.4	.2

53

TABLE IIB

AVERAGE NUMBER OF VISITS OF CORPORATE RECRUITERS TO SCHOOLS
WITH ENROLLMENTS BETWEEN 5,000 AND 9,999, WITH
VARYING JEWISH ENROLLMENTS
1972-1974

% of Undergraduate Enrollment that is Jewish	"Fortune's" top industrial firms top 100	next 400	Insurance Companies	Banks	"Fortune's" top 50 Public Utilities	Other Public Utilities
Under 10	17.9	13.9	10.3	4.7	1.7	2.1
10 - 19.9	23.8	17.5	12.0	5.8	1.8	1.3
20 - 29.9	15.5	17.5	11.5	8.0	3.5	1.0
30 & over	11.5	6.8	8.3	4.8	.8	.3

54

TABLE IIC

AVERAGE NUMBER OF VISITS OF CORPORATE RECRUITERS TO SCHOOLS
WITH ENROLLMENTS OF 10,000 AND OVER, WITH
VARYING JEWISH ENROLLMENTS

| % of Undergraduate Enrollment that is Jewish | "Fortune's" top industrial firms | | Insurance Companies | Banks | "Fortune's" top 50 Public Utilities | Other Public Utilities |
	top 100	next 400				
Under 10	31.5	34.6	13.0	9.3	3.1	3.0
10 - 19.9	40.0	42.1	10.6	5.6	6.4	4.0
20 - 29.9	31.3	29.3	10.0	8.3	2.7	.7
30 & over	10.0	8.4	10.1	3.8	1.3	.3

55

illustrates this point. Langer told us that close to half of all Morgan's management trainees established initial contact with the bank at campus interviews. When we noted that Morgan did not recruit at any branch of the City University, Langer replied that any enterprising graduate could just "hop on the subway and come to the bank for an interview." Or, he could send in his resume. "Do you get many resumes?" Langer laughed, then estimated that there were weeks when several hundred resumes "came over the transom." He also noted that about half the bank's management trainees were hired after having received a personal recommendation.

If half established initial contact through campus recruiters and the other half through personal recommendations, what percentage was hired after sending in a resume or "hopping on the subway"? We pressed this point, but Langer kept insisting that he didn't know what we were getting at. What we wanted to know was why Jewish graduates of the City University didn't have a chance of getting past the "no Jews need apply" signs that might just as well be posted outside the doors of Morgan Guaranty.

A second refinement of Table I must appreciate that several firms account for a large proportion of the visits made to the 20 heavily Jewish schools. For example, IBM visited ten of these schools, while Xerox went to nine. If these two firms as well as 31 others were excluded from the industrial corporations under consideration, we could get a much more accurate picture of the recruiting patterns of the other 467 firms.[5] We will do this in two stages: in Table IIIA, B, and C, we have eliminated first 17 of the most active corporate recruiters, and then an additional 16 firms. These firms are listed in Table IIIA.

We will now be able to compare the results shown in Tables A, B, and C with those of Tables IIA, B, and C. The averages shown in Tables IIIA, B, and C, are, of course, somewhat lower, due to the exclusion of the most active recruiters.

This analysis is limited to industrial firms because firms in the other categories provide less suitable data. It is apparent that insurance companies are recruiting at most schools, whether heavily Jewish or not. Banks limit their recruitment effort to schools with low Jewish enrollments.

TABLE IIIA

MODIFIED (a) AVERAGE NUMBER OF VISITS OF CORPORATION RECRUITERS TO SCHOOLS WITH ENROLLMENTS UNDER 5,000, WITH VARYING JEWISH ENROLLMENTS 1972-1974

"Fortune's" top industrial firms

% of Undergraduate Enrollment that is Jewish	b 86 of top 100	c 397 of next 400	d 78 of top 100	e 389 of next 400
Under 10	5.0	6.9	4.2	6.5
10 – 19.9	3.6	6.0	3.0	5.5
20 – 29.9	8.0	9.9	6.0	9.3
30 & over	3.2	4.2	2.1	3.6

a) As explained in the text, Tables IIIA, B, and C are modifications of Tables IIA, B, and C. The average number of visits in each category in this table and the next two tables by the elimination of the firms listed in notes b, c, d, and e.

b) The following firms have been eliminated from consideration: Bethlehem, DuPont, Exxon, Firestone, Ford, General Electric, IBM, Mobil, Procter & Gamble, Raytheon, Texaco, United Aircraft, Westinghouse and Xerox.

c) The following firms have been eliminated from consideration: Burroughs, Merck, and Upjohn.

d) In addition to the firms listed in note b, the following firms have been eliminated from consideration: Allied Chemical, Atlantic Richfield, Chrysler, General Dynamics, B. F. Goodrich, R. J. Reynolds, Standard Oil of California, and Union Carbide.

e) In addition to the firms listed in note c, the following firms have been eliminated from consideration: Combustion Engineering, R. Donnelley, M. Lowenstein, Naval Resale Systems, Rohm & Haas, Texas Instruments, and United Merchants and Manufacturers.

57

TABLE IIIB

MODIFIED (a) AVERAGE NUMBER OF VISITS OF CORPORATE RECRUITERS TO SCHOOLS WITH ENROLLMENTS BETWEEN 5,000 AND 9,999, WITH VARYING JEWISH ENROLLMENTS 1972-1974

"Fortune's" top industrial firms

% of Undergraduate Enrollment that is Jewish	b 86 of top 100	c 397 of next 400	d 78 of top 100	e 389 of next 400
Under 10	10.7	12.6	8.9	12.0
10 - 19.9	21.0	21.0	18.3	20.0
20 - 29.9	9.0	15.5	7.0	15.0
30 & over	6.3	6.0	5.0	3.8

a) As explained in the text, Tables IIIA, B, and C are modifications of Tables IIA, B, and C. The average number of visits in each category in this table and the next two tables by the elimination of the firms listed in notes b, c, d, and e.

b) The following firms have been eliminated from consideration: Bethlehem, DuPont, Exxon, Firestone, Ford, General Electric, IBM, Mobil, Procter & Gamble, Raytheon, Texaco, United Aircraft, Westinghouse and Xerox.

c) The following firms have been eliminated from consideration: Burroughs, Merck, and Upjohn.

d) In addition to the firms listed in note b, the following firms have been eliminated from consideration: Allied Chemical, Atlantic Richfield, Chrysler, General Dynamics, B. F. Goodrich, R. J. Reynolds, Standard Oil of California, and Union Carbide.

e) In addition to the firms listed in note c, the following firms have been eliminated from consideration: Combustion Engineering, R. Donnelley, M. Lowenstein, Naval Resale Systems, Rohm & Haas, Texas Instruments, and United Merchants and Manufacturers.

TABLE IIIC

MODIFIED (a) AVERAGE NUMBER OF VISITS OF CORPORATE RECRUITERS TO SCHOOLS WITH ENROLLMENTS OF 10,000 AND OVER, WITH VARYING JEWISH ENROLLMENTS 1972-1974

"Fortune's" top industrial firms

% of Undergraduate Enrollment that is Jewish	b 86 of top 100	c 397 of next 400	d 78 of top 100	e 389 of next 400
Under 10	22.7	33.5	20.0	32.0
10 - 19.9	29.9	40.1	25.0	37.7
20 - 29.9	20.3	27.0	16.3	24.7
30 & over	4.9	6.5	3.0	5.1

a) As explained in the text, Tables IIIA, B, and C are modifications of Tables IIA, B, and C. The average number of visits in each category in this table and the next two tables by the elimination of the firms listed in notes b, c, d, and e.

b) The following firms have been eliminated from consideration: Bethlehem, DuPont, Exxon, Firestone, Ford, General Electric, IBM, Mobil, Procter & Gamble, Raytheon, Texaco, United Aircraft, Westinghouse and Xerox.

c) The following firms have been eliminated from consideration: Burroughs, Merck, and Upjohn.

d) In addition to the firms listed in note b, the following firms have been eliminated from consideration: Allied Chemical, Atlantic Richfield, Chrysler, General Dynamics, B. F. Goodrich, R. J. Reynolds, Standard Oil of California, and Union Carbide.

e) In addition to the firms listed in note c, the following firms have been eliminated from consideration: Combustion Engineering, R. Donnelley, M. Lowenstein, Naval Resale Systems, Rohm & Haas, Texas Instruments, and United Merchants and Manufacturers.

An examination of the corresponding parts of
Tables II and III reveals the effects of the exclusion
of the most active corporate recruiters. Now we find,
however, that in every case, there is a marked decline
in the average number of visits made to schools with
enrollments that are over 30 per cent Jewish. In other
words, aside from a handful of firms that recruit
widely, perhaps over 90 per cent of the large industrial firms avoid heavily Jewish colleges.

Comparing Table IIA and IIIA, one can observe
somewhat sharper declines in the latter table as Jewish
enrollment passes the 30 per cent mark. The decline
becomes still sharper when one compares Tables IIB and
IIIB. Apparently, then, as the size of college enrollment rises, corporate avoidance of Jewish schools
becomes still more obvious when we look at Table IIC
and IIIC. There is a precipitous decline at the 30
per cent mark, but it is even more spectacular in the
latter table.

Fortune's top 500 industrial firms made 318 visits
to colleges that were at least 39 per cent Jewish;
165 (51.9 per cent) of these visits were accounted
for by the 33 firms listed in Table IIIA. That means
that a large majority of the remaining 467 companies
did not send a representative to even one college which
had a substantial Jewish enrollment.

D. Preliminary Conclusion

The implications of these results will be
investigated more fully in Chapter IX, in conjunction
with those of the next four chapters. In this
chapter we have answered the question whether the
large industrial corporations, insurance companies,
banks and public utilities were avoiding schools
with high Jewish enrollments. The evidence is clear:
the "Jewish" schools are systematically avoided.
Although the recruiting patterns of insurance companies
are more ambiguous, earlier studies (summarized in
Chapter III) suggest that these recruiters are interviewing prospective Jewish salesmen rather than
administrators.

There is a certain consistency to the data
presented so far. We cannot point a finger at any
particular corporation just yet, but we can observe

a pervasive pattern of avoidance of "Jewish" colleges. When we look at the total of 467 corporations which sent so few recruiters to these colleges, we cannot single out any particular corporation and promounce it guilty. We can say, however, that as a group, indeed, as a system, the corporate structure of America is anti-Semitic.

Having examined corporate recruiting patterns from the perspective of various colleges, we shall now look at the recruitment records of individual corporations. To some extent, then, the analysis of the following chapter is an extension of that begun in the present one. And now we ask, "Which corporations are avoiding 'Jewish' schools?"

Chapter Notes

1. A slightly different version of this chapter appears as "Bias in U.S. Big Business Recruitment," in Patterns of Prejudice, Vol. 101 No. 5, September-October, 1976.

2. See Appendix at end of book, Section A.

3. The tipping point was discussed in a Yale Law Journal article in reference to the hiring policies of many large law firms. Only a certain number of openings can safely be filled before the firm is pushed past the tipping point and known as a Jewish firm. See The Editors of the Yale Law Journal, "The Jewish Law Student and New York Jobs -- Discriminatory Effects in Law Firm Hiring Practices," The Yale Law Journal, Vol. 73, No. 4, March 1964, p. 650.

4. The inside-outside dichotomy is documented by the Anti-Defamation League in Rights, Vol. 7, 1968. See Chapter III, Section C.

5. Just making a corporate visit to a "Jewish" school does not of course guarantee that any Jews will get job offers. In fact, as we'll discuss in Chapter VII, at any given college, a gentile graduate is three times more likely than his Jewish classmate to be employed by a large corporation.

CHAPTER V

LOOKING AT INDIVIDUAL FIRMS' RECRUITMENT PATTERNS

A. Introduction

Now we are ready to name names and to assess the
performance of the corporate recruiters within the
context of probability analysis. We will now take
a closer look at companies that seem to avoid "Jewish"
schools. How likely is it, statistically, for a
company to send recruiters to 15 or 20 schools and
not happen to include even one with a substantial
Jewish enrollment?

We are continuing to examine corporate recruiting patterns, but these firms will no longer be
anonymous. This analysis parallels that of the
previous chapter, but examines the recruiting records
of specific firms. We will temporarily disregard
the Fortune classifications, but most of the companies
are readily recognizable.

The mere fact that a corporation does not recruit

at schools with large Jewish enrollments does not necessarily evidence anti-Semitism. We cannot of course infer that a corporation is anti-Semitic simply because it did not recruit at any schools with large Jewish enrollments. A firm may have done little or no recruiting or perhaps recruited only in its own locale. The company might have sought only engineering graduates or perhaps had more exotic requirements, such as a major in agronomics or biostatistics. It's also remotely possible that the firm skipped over all the Jewish schools by chance.

For many of the large companies, no pattern can be established, because their recruiting efforts are minimal. Nearly 300 corporations recruited actively on college campuses. However, we have selected the recruitment schedules of 139 firms for further analysis because none of these firms sent a representative to more than four substantially Jewish schools on our list.

B. The Data

The corporations listed in Table I made not one recruitment visit to a campus with 30 per cent or more Jewish enrollment, yet they recruited at eight or more colleges. Both the Goodyear corporation and Pittsburgh Plate Glass Industries (PPG) managed to visit 55 colleges without stopping at even one "Jewish" school. Would it be fair to suspect conscious or unconscious anti-Semitism in this pattern?

Corporations listed in Tables II and III each visited one, two, three or four Jewish schools. Their total campus recruiting effort is given to show their apparent preference for schools with low Jewish enrollments.

Impressionistically, we note that well-known firms with active recruitment schedules happened to visit few Jewish schools or none. How likely is it, statistically, that these companies followed this recruiting pattern without going out of their way to avoid the Jewish schools?

To answer this question, a probability model can be set up as easily as one would calculate the odds of drawing various hands from a deck of cards. For example, the chances of drawing two kings in a

TABLE I

COMPANIES RECRUITING AT NO "JEWISH" COLLEGES*
1972-1973

Company	Total Number of Colleges Visited	Company	Total Number of Colleges Visited
Goodyear	55	American Air Filter	21
PPG	55	Fluor Corp.	21
Schlumberg Well Service	48	National Steel	21
Shell Oil	38	Whirlpool	21
Armco Steel	34	Westvaco	20
Borg-Warner	34	Dayton's	19
Charmin	33	Jewel Companies	19
Amoco Chemicals	30	Walker Mfg. Co.	19
Square "D"	29	Del Monte	18
Ethyl Corp.	27	Gates Rubber Co.	18
Alcoa	26	LTV	18
Cities Service	25	Control Data	17
Union Oil	25	Collins Radio	16
Oscar Mayer	24	Hercules	16
U.S. Gypsum	23	American Can	15
Deere	22	Baxter Labs	15
George A. Hormel	22	Leeds & Northrup	15
Phillips Petroleum	22	Ohio Edison	15
Turner Construction Co.	22	The Kroger Co.	15
		Brunswick	14

TABLE I - Continued

Company	Total Number of Colleges Visited	Company	Total Number of Colleges Visited
Humble Oil	14	Pennzoil	11
Marathon Oil	14	Agway	10
Northrop	14	American Enka	10
Reynolds Metals	14	Ceco Corp.	10
Tektronix	14	Cummins Engine	9
Parke Davis	13	Johns-Manville	9
Swift	13	M.W. Kellogg	9
Addressograph-Multigraph	12	Kraft Foods	9
Bell & Howell	12	Standard Brands	9
Kaiser	12	Weyerhaeuser	9
Detroit Edison	11	Simmons	8

* Schools with at least 30 per cent Jewish enrollment

TABLE II

COMPANIES RECRUITING AT ONE "JEWISH" COLLEGE
1972-1973

Company	Total Number of Colleges Visited	Company	Total Number of Colleges Visited
Monsanto	54	NCR	27
Continental Oil	52	Gulf Oil	26
Babcock & Wilcox	51	Owens-Corning	26
Motorola	48	Continental Can	24
Allis Chalmers	45	Koppers	24
Diamond Shamrock	44	Owens-Illinois	24
Dow	44	Intel	22
Stauffer	44	Pfizer	22
General Motors	40	Pittsburgh-Des Moines	22
Anaconda	36	Sun Oil	22
Eaton	36	American Motors	21
Union Oil	36	Montgomery Ward	21
Chicago Bridge & Iron	33	International Paper	19
Ingersoll Rand	32	Sherwin Williams	19
Jones & Laughlin	31	Hallmark	18
Republic Steel	29	Yellow Freight Systems	18
Boeing	28	Getty Oil	17
U.S. Steel	28	Lockheed	17
Carnation	27	Johnson & Johnson	16
FMC	27		

TABLE II -- Continued

Company	Total Number of Colleges Visited	Company	Total Number of Colleges Visited
Carrier	15	Philip Morris	11
TRW	15	Union Trust (Maryland)	11
International Harvester	12	Coca-Cola	9

TABLE IIIA

COMPANIES RECRUITING AT TWO, THREE, AND FOUR
"JEWISH" COLLEGES
1972-1973

Companies Recruiting at <u>Two</u> "Jewish Colleges:

Company	Total Number of Colleges Visited	Company	Total Number of Colleges Visited
Sears	89	Foster Wheeler	27
K Mart	61	General Mills	26
Trane	48	Sperry Rand	26
Corning Glass	47	Union Camp	26
Armstrong Cork	42	Sea-Land Service	25
Cargill	42	Continental Illinois Bank	23
F.W. Woolworth	40	Caterpillar	21
Johnson Controls	34	Martin Marietta	21
Universal Oil	34	McDonnell Aircraft	21
Minneapolis Honeywell	32	American Cyanamid	18
Magnavox	31	Singer	18
Mellon National Bank	31	Ebasco Services	17

Companies Recruiting at <u>Three</u> "Jewish" Colleges:

Company	Total Number of Colleges Visited	Company	Total Number of Colleges Visited
Rockwell International	61	Bechtel	34
Wallace Business Forms	46	Norton	31
		Ortho	30
Hewlett-Packard	38		

TABLE IIIB

Companies Recruiting at <u>Four</u> "Jewish" Colleges:

Company	Total Number of Colleges Visited	Company	Total Number of Colleges Visited
Celanese	60	J.C. Penney	60

row (without replacing them in the deck) would be 4/52 x 3/51 is 12/2652 or .0045 (45 in 10,000). Using our sample of 170 colleges (our deck) and the 21 Jewish colleges (our kings), it is a simple process to calculate the chances of missing all or most of the Jewish schools.

What is the probability, then, that a corporate recruiter, picking colleges without regard to their level of Jewish enrollment, would visit so few Jewish colleges? What is the probability that a corporation might recruit at, say, 25 colleges, as did Cities Service, and yet not happen to hit even one Jewish college? As we can see in Table IV, the probability of this happening by chance is only .281. In other words, the chances that a corporate recruiter would make such selections at random are only 28 in 1,000 (See Appendix C for the formulas used).

We can set up a probability model along these lines. What is the probability that a corporate recruiter, picking colleges at random (from a religious perspective), would visit so few Jewish colleges?

What we shall be seeing in the next three tables are the probabilities that these corporations were not avoiding Jewish schools. And as we shall see, these probabilities are not high.

C. Analysis of the Data

What, then, do these figures mean? Although it would not be thoroughly legitimate to draw any conclusion about individual companies, by taking a few examples, we can draw certain inferences from the probability data.

If a company were to select colleges at random (without regard to the religious composition of the student bodies), it would be expected to attain a probability score of .5000 (or 50%). This is analogous to flipping a coin several times: one would expect to get heads approximately 50% of the time. What if you flipped a coin 50 times but got only 10 heads (probability score of .044). Is the coin crooked? What if you got only 5 heads (probability score of .101)? At some point one would begin

71

TABLE IV

PROBABILITIES COMPANIES RANDOMLY AVOIDED ALL "JEWISH" COLLEGES 1972-1973

Company	Probability	Company	Probability
Goodyear	.0002	American Air Filter	.0519
PPG	.0002	Fluor Corp.	.0519
Schlumberger Well Service	.0005	National Steel	.0519
Shell Oil	.0034	Whirlpool	.0519
Armco Steel	.0066	Timken	.0603
Borg-Warner	.0066	Westvaco	.0603
Amoco Chemicals	.0127	Dayton's	.0701
Square "D"	.0149	Jewel Companies	.0701
Ethyl Corp.	.0205	Walker Mfg. Co.	.0701
Alcoa	.0240	Del Monte	.0813
Charmin	.0281	Gates Rubber Co.	.0813
Cities Service	.0281	LTV	.0813
Union Oil	.0281	Control Data	.0942
Oscar Mayer	.0328	Collins Radio	.1091
U.S. Gypsum	.0383	Hercules	.1091
Deere	.0446	American Can	.1262
George A. Hormel	.0446	Baxter Labs	.1262
Phillips Petroleum	.0446	The Kroger Co.	.1262
Turner Construction Co.	.0446	Ohio Edison	.1262

TABLE IV -- Continued

Company	Probability	Company	Probability
Leeds & Northrup	.1262	Detroit Edison	.2235
Brunswick	.1458	Pennzoil	.2235
Humble Oil	.1458	Agway	.2573
Marathon Oil	.1458	American Enka	.2573
Northrop	.1458	Ceco Corp.	.2573
Reynolds Metals	.1458	Cummins Engine	.2959
Tektronix	.1458	Johns-Manville	.2959
Parke Davis	.1683	M.W. Kellogg	.2959
Swift	.1683	Kraft Foods	.2959
Addressograph-Multigraph	.1941	Standard Brands	.2959
Bell & Howell	.1941	Weyerhaeuser	.2959
Kaiser	.1941	Simmons	.3400

TABLE V

PROBABILITIES COMPANIES RANDOMLY AVOIDED ALL BUT ONE "JEWISH" COLLEGE
1972-1973

Company	Probability	Company	Probability
Monsanto	.0009	FMC	.0437
Continental Oil	.0013	NCR	.0437
Babcock & Wilcox	.0015	Gulf Oil	.0490
Motorola	.0024	Owens-Corning	.0490
Allis Chalmers	.0038	Continental Can	.0611
Diamond Shamrock	.0045	Koppers	.0611
Dow	.0045	Owens-Illinois	.0611
Stauffer	.0045	Intel	.0754
General Motors	.0081	Pfizer	.0754
Anaconda	.0141	Pittsburgh-Des Moines	.0754
Eaton	.0141	Sun Oil	.0754
Union Oil	.0141	American Motors	.0834
Chicago Bridge & Iron	.0210	Montgomery Ward	.0834
Ingersoll-Rand	.0238	International Paper	.1011
Jones & Laughlin	.0270	Sherwin Williams	.1011
Republic Steel	.0345	Hallmark	.1107
Boeing	.0389	Yellow Freight Systems	.1107
U.S. Steel	.0389	Getty Oil	.1207
Carnation	.0437		

TABLE V -- Continued

Company	Probability	Company	Probability
Lockheed	.1207	International Harvester	.1740
Johnson & Johnson	.1312	Philip Morris	.1839
Carrier	.1419	Union Trust (Maryland)	.1839
TRW	.1419	Coca-Cola	.2003

TABLE VI

PROBABILITIES COMPANIES RANDOMLY AVOIDED ALL
BUT TWO, THREE, OR FOUR "JEWISH" COLLEGES
1972–1973

Companies Recruiting at Two "Jewish" Colleges

Company	Probability	Company	Probability
Sears	.00001	General Mills	.1867
K Mart	.0027	Sperry Rand	.1867
Trane	.0193	Union Camp	.1867
Corning Glass	.0220	Sea-Land Service	.2000
Armstrong Cork	.0406		
Cargill	.0406	Continental Illinois Bank	.2266
F.W. Woolworth	.0511	Caterpillar	.2523
Johnson Controls	.0954	Martin Marietta	.2523
Universal Oil	.0954	McDonnell Aircraft	.2523
Minneapolis Honeywell	.1150	American Cyanamid	.2853
Magnavox	.1257	Singer	.2853
Mellon National Bank	.1257	Ebasco Services	.2937
Foster Wheeler	.1737		

TABLE VI -- Continued

Companies Recruiting at Three "Jewish" Colleges:

Company	Probability	Company	Probability
Rockwell International	.0107	Bechtel	.1653
Wallace Business Forms	.0630	Norton	.1956
		Ortho	.2057
Hewlett-Packard	.1259		

Companies Recruiting at Four "Jewish" Colleges:

Company	Probability	Company	Probability
Celanese	.0671	J.C. Penney	.0671

to suspect that the coin was biased.

Some of the companies listed in Tables IV to VI have exceedingly low probability scores. Such low scores are interpreted statistically as the probability that, due to chance factors, a particular unlikely event will take place. For example, the probability score of Amoco Chemicals is .0127 (see Table IV) which indicates that approximately one per cent of the time, such a low score would be due to chance factors. And the rest of the time? In 99 per cent of such cases, the cause of such infrequent recruiting at Jewish schools is due to good old fashioned anti-Semitism.

But we must not jump hastily to conclusions. There might be ameliorating factors (which will be discussed in the next section), and perhaps more important, we cannot take these probability scores as incontrovertible proof of discrimination. The point being made here is that when a corporation visits few or no Jewish colleges, this avoidance cannot be attributed to chance alone.

Some of the companies had amazingly low probability scores. Shell Oil was at .0034, Motorola at .0024, Babcock & Wilcox at .0015, Continental Oil was at .0013, Monsanto at .0009, Schlumberger Well Service at .0005, both Goodyear and PPG at .0002, while Sears had the lowest probability score -- .00001. Together these nine companies visited 496 schools, of which only six were Jewish.

When probability scores get as low as these, one is hard pressed to suggest how these companies might have gone about their recruiting without consciously avoiding the Jewish schools. We have written to each of the firms with probability scores below .05, asking the recruitment directors how they managed to follow such a biased recruitment pattern. Most did not bother to reply. Nearly all who did either pointed out they were "equal opportunity employers" or that their recruitment was so decentralized that they themselves did not have a full listing of the colleges their representatives visited.

Although these probability scores are rather low, actually, there is an upward bias incorporated into these figures. Because our sampling of colleges was designed to include those with the largest Jewish enrollments, obviously many non-Jewish colleges were excluded. Most of these excluded colleges have very low enrollments and do not constitute a major source of corporate executives. Nevertheless, had every school in the country been included in our survey (i.e., had we taken a census instead of a sample), then the resulting probability scores would have been still lower. For example, Magnavox visited 33 campuses in our sample, 2 of which were Jewish. However, the Magnavox recruiters visited an additional 14 colleges, outside our sample, and none of these was Jewish. If we calculated its probability score on the basis of 47 colleges rather than 33, that score would fall from .1257 to .0283.

Another reason why we have underestimated avoidance of Jewish colleges is that we have data from every school with a heavy Jewish enrollment, but only a 70% return from other schools. Since we have not received corroborating data from every corporation, it was necessary in some cases to list only data received from the colleges. Therefore, 100% of the Jewish schools, but only 70% of the non-Jewish schools, provided data, so the probability scores are based on somewhat underestimated visits to non-Jewish schools. To the degree that these visits are underestimated, the probability scores are overestimated.

We have been looking at corporate recruitment as if the choices of schools were made at random, but of course recruiters have some criteria for selection. Most corporations concentrate their recruitment in their own geographic region, while others are interested in graduates who have specific majors. Academic prowess may be an additional consideration.

D. Regional Recruiting Patterns

In a survey of 216 corporations, we found that about two-thirds confined their campus visits largely to their own geographic regions. One would not expect, for example, the Eastern campuses (many of which are Jewish) to be visited by more than a few California firms. Recruiting directors for these 216 firms were asked how they initially contacted their recently-hired college graduates. The results, shown in Table VII, indicate that over 70 per cent had their first interviews on campus. Although one can always

TABLE VII

HOW RECENTLY HIRED COLLEGE GRADUATES
WERE INITIALLY CONTACTED
1972-1974

Initial Contact	Percentage Share
Campus Interview	70.5%
Recommended by a current employee	7.0%
Sent unsolicited resume	12.9%
Responded to ad in College Placement Annual, professional journal or newspaper	9.7%

apply directly to any company, it appears that the main avenue of prospective employment is the campus interview.[1]

Some corporations -- IBM, Xerox, and F.W. Woolworth, for example -- recruit at schools in almost every state, while others, most notably banks and public utilities, confine their recruiting efforts mainly to the regions in which they are situated. There is also a substantial amount of local recruitment, i.e., recruiting within a hundred mile radius of the corporate headquarters.

Apparently New York City and its environs are practically off limits to corporate recruiters. This is rather surprising because there are roughly 65 colleges within easy commuting distance of Times Square. Of course this area also has the largest concentration of Jews in the world.

Perhaps it's not necessary for the corporations to recruit in New York, since local students could easily visit the headquarters of several large corporations. However, there is considerable evidence that this is not a feasible course of action for most students. As was indicated in Table VIII, above, by far the largest percentage of new employees is initially contacted at campus interviews. Moreover, while the New York corporations are not doing very much local recruiting, this is not true of firms based in other large cities. This is apparent when we compare the recruitment patterns of New York firms with those based in Chicago, Cleveland and Detroit, as we have done in Table VIII below.

Table VIII makes it quite clear that corporations in the New York area recruit much less intensively on a local basis than those with headquarters in other major cities. While local campus visits constitute only 10.8% of total visits made by New York firms, the figures for Chicago, Cleveland, and Detroit are 20.3%, 33.3%, and 23.3%, respectively. Furthermore, the New York figures may even be over-stated, since a relatively high proportion of New York area colleges are included in this survey.

Let's look at the record. Most corporations recruit much more intensively in their immediate vicinity than they do on a nationwide basis. Firms based in or near large cities generally do at least 20 per cent of their recruiting at local schools.

81

TABLE VIII

LOCAL AND OUT-OF-TOWN CAMPUS VISITS BY RECRUITERS FROM SELECTED CHICAGO, CLEVELAND DETROIT AND NEW YORK FIRMS
1972-1973

Chicago Firms

Firm	Local Visits*	Out-of-Town Visits
Bell & Howell	7	5
Borg-Warner	8	26
Brunswick	5	9
Chicago Iron & Bridge	3	31
Continental Illinois	8	17
FMC	3	26
International Harvestor	3	10
Jewel Companies	6	13
Montgomery Ward	3	19
Motorola	5	44
Quaker Oats	3	6
Swift	3	10
U.S. Gypsum	4	19

* Local visits as a % of total visits: 20.3%

TABLE VIII -- Continued

Cleveland Firms

Firm	Local Visits*	Out-of-Town Visits
Addressograph-Multigraph	3	9
Diamond Shamrock	17	28
Eaton	13	24
Sherwin-Williams	9	11
TRW	1	14

* Local visits as a % of total visits: 33.3%

Detroit Firms

Firm	Local Visits*	Out-of-Town Visits
American Motors	5	17
Amoco Chemicals	2	28
General Motors	7	34
Parke Davis	6	7

* Local visits as a % of total visits: 23.3%

TABLE VIII -- Continued

New York Firms

Firm	Local Visits*	Out-of-Town Visits
American Can	2	13
American Cyanamid	4	14
Anaconda	1	32
Babcock & Wilcox	2	50
Cities Service	0	25
Continental Oil	3	50
Ebasco	6	12
First National City Bank	11	20
Foster Wheeler	4	25
Ingersoll-Rand	3	30
International Paper	2	18
Johnson & Johnson	2	15
Magnavox	1	32
Martin Marietta	1	22
Ortho	4	27
J.C. Penney	6	58
Pfizer	3	20
Philip Morris	2	10
St. Regis	1	13
Sea Land Service	3	22
Singer	3	17

84

TABLE VIII -- Continued

Firms	Local Visits*	Out-of-Town Visits
Sperry Rand	3	25
Standard Brands	1	8
Stauffer	4	41
Turner Construction	3	19
Union Camp	3	12
Westvaco	0	20
F.W. Woolworth	5	36

* Local visits as a % of total visits: 10.8%

Given the concentration of Jewish schools in the New York area, it would seem that many of these schools would be visited.

Of all the schools visited by the New York-based corporations, 4.6 per cent were substantially Jewish; the 110 out-of-town corporations had an even lower average -- 2.4 per cent. In our sample, only 21 of the 170 schools were Jewish, while 11 of the 24 schools within 50 miles of New York were Jewish. If all schools visited had been selected on a random basis, then obviously the Jewish colleges would have received many more recruiters.

New York City has the world's largest concentration of educated Jews as well as the largest concentration of corporate headquarters. Furthermore, most of the "Jewish" colleges in our sample are in the New York area. Let's take a look at the recruitment patterns of large New York-based firms.

The relatively low number of visits to New York City schools is perhaps indicative of a prejudice not against Jews, but against the city itself. Whatever the evils of New York, whether real or imagined, it is understandable that some corporations would associate the graduates of the city's schools with these evils. Moreover, the large proportion of Jewish college graduates hardly diminishes corporate misgivings about recruiting at these schools.

Very often, corporations need to recruit students who have majored in particular fields, most notably engineering. While there are several Jewish schools that turn out engineering graduates, it is certainly possible for them to have been avoided by chance rather than anti-Semitic design. However, even corporations seeking engineers must also hire accountants, finance majors, and other non-engineering graduates. In fairness to companies with specialized needs, we will note that the following firms have indicated an interest in recruiting only engineers.

Academic standing does not appear to have any bearing on corporate recruitment. The state universities are most assiduously cultivated by corporate recruiters, while Ivy League schools are as frequently visited as other less prestigious private colleges. Several of the Jewish schools are among those with high academic standing -- Columbia, Yale, Brandeis and Washington University, for example -- but if the

TABLE IX

RECRUITING RECORDS OF COMPANIES BASED IN THE
NEW YORK CITY VICINITY*
1972-1973

Company	Visits to schools with enrollments less than 30% Jewish	more than 30% Jewish	Probability of Random Avoidance
Continental Oil	52	1	.0013
Babcock & Wilcox	51	1	.0015
Stauffer	44	1	.0045
Rockwell International	61	3	.0107
Anaconda	35	1	.0141
Ingersoll Rand	32	1	.0238
Cities Service	25	0	.0281
U.S. Steel	28	1	.0389
Turner Construction Co.	22	0	.0446
F. W. Woolworth	40	2	.0511
Westvaco	20	0	.0603
Celanese	60	4	.0671
J.C. Penney	60	4	.0671
Pfizer	22	1	.0754
International Paper	19	1	.1011
Magnavox	31	2	.1257
American Can	15	0	.1262

TABLE IX -- Continued

Company	Visits to schools with enrollments less than 30% Jewish	more than 30% Jewish	Probability of Random Avoidance
Johnson & Johnson	16	1	.1312
Foster Wheeler	27	2	.1737
Philip Morris	11	1	.1839
Sperry Rand	26	2	.1867
Union Camp	26	2	.1867
Sea-Land Service	25	2	.2000
Ortho	30	3	.2057
Martin Marietta	21	2	.2523
American Cyanamid	18	2	.2853
Singer	18	2	.2853
Ebasco Services	17	2	.2937
Standard Brands	9	0	.2959
Simmons	8	0	.3400

TABLE X

FIRMS SEEKING ONLY ENGINEERS
1972-1973

Amoco Chemicals*

Charmin*

Fluor

Pittsburgh-Des Moines

Turner Construction

Westvaco*

* Considers other majors if closely related to
engineering

Source: In addition to our survey of 170 colleges,
we found considerable data on corporate preferences
in The College Placement Council, College Placement
Annual 1973 (Bethlehem, Pa.: The College Placement
Council, 1973).

corporations are not seeking out intellectuals, then it would appear that <u>Jewish</u> intellectuals might have more than one strike against them.

A particularly glaring example of corporate avoidance of "Jewish" schools is the City University of New York. Recruiters assiduously avoid even the well-regarded four-year colleges (Brooklyn, City, Hunter, Lehman, and Queens). Those who claim that open enrollment[2] has caused this avoidance are mistaken, because there were few recruiters before this policy.

E. Conclusions

The interpretation of the data on corporate recruitment is most difficult. It would be best to set limits on the types of conclusions that will be reached. Clearly, we cannot conclude, on the basis of the probability models of this chapter, that any of the companies mentioned are engaged in conscious efforts to avoid Jewish applicants. On the other hand, we can validly reach a minimal conclusion -- that the companies in question have not been actively recruiting at schools with large Jewish enrollments.

Perhaps, then, the truth lies somewhere in between. Very possibly certain individuals on a middle or lower management level have consciously or unconsciously set up recruiting schedules which avoid Jewish schools. Even in cases where top management issues orders that the best qualified applicants be hired and promoted, these orders can easily be subverted by almost any lower level manager.

Important, but more difficult to appraise, are the social backgrounds of college recruiters, personnel officials, and department heads participating in the hiring process. Members of a racial, religious, or ethnic group probably tend to favor other members of their own groups. Graduates of certain schools are undoubtedly favored over those who studied elsewhere. The favored schools are not necessarily better, just more familiar. And surely corporate recruiters make more of an effort to visit their alma maters than any other schools, however worthy.

Finally, the role of the alumni, fraternities, and the old boy system should not go unmentioned.

Surely there are hundreds of thousands of corporate executives who obtained their positions through this informal recruitment network. The role of fraternities, although somewhat revived since the Sixties, is no longer an important avenue of employment. The old boy network, however, plays a continuing role in placing people from illustrious families with prestigious firms, most notably investment banks.[3] These informal hiring systems have worked against Jews, since very few have gone to the Midwestern state universities (where the alumni exert the greatest influence), joined the "right" fraternities, or had the proper old boy pedigree.

The conclusion is inescapable that Jews are being excluded from large sectors of American industry. At this point we're not presuming to speculate on intent. Statisticians define a nonrandom sample as "biased." If all members of a population do not have an equal chance of being selected in a sample, then the results of that sample are biased. The person doing the sampling is not necessarily biased, but he is judged by his results. Unless he takes every precaution to make his selections completely random (in this case with regard to religious composition), he might well have an unrepresentative and therefore biased sample.

The personnel director is largely responsible for the stream of recruits considered for jobs in a company. Although he may have been completely unprejudiced, he may have unconsciously provided a disproportionate number of WASP males or Irish Catholics, or whatever, simply because he did not take the necessary steps to insure that a wide cross-section of job-seekers would apply. Surely few personnel directors make this effort, if we judge their firms by the recruitment schedules at the time of this survey.

Chapter Notes

1. The second way to get a job with a major corporation is through a personal recommendation. See Chapter IV, Section C.

2. Open enrollment guarantees admission to every New York City high school graduate. However, most of these students are placed in community colleges, rather than four-year schools.

3. See David Halberstam, <u>The Best and the Brightest</u>, (New York: Random House, 1972), especially Chapters 1 - 6.

CHAPTER VI

HIRING THROUGH EMPLOYMENT AGENCIES AND EXECUTIVE SEARCH FIRMS

A. Earlier Surveys

There are three ways of getting a job -- applying
directly, being recruited, or going to an employment
agency.[1] Employment agencies are more important for
white collar jobs than for college graduate entry
positions, but their policies presumably reflect
those of the companies they serve.

To do business, employment agencies must send
their most desirable applicants. Would it be all
right to send a Black or a Jew for this job? This
question arose so frequently that it became useful
to develop this code: one (WASP), two (Irish
Catholic), three (Jew) and four (Negro).

Several employment agency studies done by the
Anti-Defamation League in the '50's and '60's indicated a strong anti-Semitic bias, our own findings

a 1975 survey of some 450 employment agencies confirmed this bias, though it is probably less severe than it had been 10 or 15 years ago.

The acceptance by employment of discriminatory job orders -- e.g., "Send me a Nordic-type secretary," was the gauge by which the earlier studies measured the extent of discrimination. In some cases, the researcher called an agency and attempted to place an order for a non-Jewish worker. In others, the employment agencies themselves disclosed the percentage of job orders they got specifying that no Jews were wanted.

Lois Waldman summarizing the results of three ADL surveys done in the 1950's.[2] The first, done in 1951, analyzed job orders placed with the Los Angeles offices of the California Public Employment Service. Fully 50 per cent of the management and professional orders and 27 per cent of the clerical orders were found to discriminate against Jews. Another study done two years later in Chicago found that 27 per cent of the job orders placed with private employment agencies specified "no Jews." The results of a third study are shown in Table I.

Obviously Catholic and Protestant applicants fared better than Jewish applicants. Considering that many companies openly placed discriminatory job orders with employment agencies, it was not surprising that Jews had more difficulty finding jobs.

In 1955 the ADL found that 125 of 129 California employment agencies still accepted telephoned job orders containing discriminatory specifications.[3] And as late as 1964, 32 of 34 Phoenix employment agencies and 41 of 42 Atlanta agencies accepted such orders.[4]

The American Jewish Congress has also been active in testing employment agencies. In 1955, 222 New York City agencies were called in an attempt to place an order for a white Protestant stenographer. In this study, 70.3 per cent accepted this order. Similar studies disclosed acceptance rates of 88.4 per cent in 1946, 64.2 per cent in 1949, and 65.0 per cent in 1952.[5]

TABLE I

OPPORTUNITY OF PLACEMENT OF JEWISH AND NON-JEWISH
JOB-SEEKERS APPLYING TO A CHICAGO (PRIVATE)
EMPLOYMENT AGENCY*, 1955

Religion	Percentage of Applicants	Percentage of Placements
Protestant	38.3%	46.3%
Catholic	37.0	39.2
Jewish	16.2	9.2

* Total of 5,582 applicants

Source: Lois Waldman, "Employment Discrimination
Against Jews in the United States -- 1955," Jewish
Social Studies, Vol. 18, No. 3, July, 1956

TABLE II

SURVEY OF PRIVATE EMPLOYMENT AGENCIES IN
SIX SELECTED CITIES
1964

City	Number of Agencies Surveyed	Number Accepting Order	Percentage Accepting
Chicago	106	101	95%
Kansas City	55	49	95
Los Angeles	77	66	86
Miami	38	38	100
New York	91	60	67
Omaha	14	14	100

Source: Anti-Defamation League, ADL Bulletin, Vol. 24, No. 3, May 1967, p. 6.

B. Our Survey

Employment agencies and executive search firms occupy a unique position in the hiring process, because they are well situated to observe any anti-Semitic attitudes and practices among their client firms. In March 1975, we sent questionnaires to 450 executive recruiting firms. Of these, 321 were based in New York City, 84 in Los Angeles, and 45 in Philadelphia -- the cities with the largest concentrations of Jewish college graduates in the nation. Seventy-seven of the firms were out of business by the time of the survey. Of the remaining 373 firms, 124 (33.2 per cent) responded. Twenty-one indicated that they were involved in placing highly skilled technical personnel and consequently encountered little anti-Semitism. An additional 18 recruiters stated that they had not received any discriminatory job orders in at least the last five to ten years. Two in fact, stated, "You are beating a dead horse."

Nevertheless, there was considerable evidence of continuing anti-Semitic hiring practices. There were eight positive responses to the first question: "Do any of the employers still use the numbered code of (1) WASP, (2) Catholic, (3) Jew, and (4) Black?" Eighteen firms responded positively to the second question: "Do you receive any job orders specifically requesting a non-Jew?" In two cases , however, the client needed someone to work Saturdays, and so was merely requesting a non-Sabbath observer.

In answer to: "Would you send a Jewish applicant to every company you deal with?" 20 firms responded negatively. This indicated a presumed prejudice on the part of prospective employers, rather than great candor on the part of the executive placement firms.

The responses to these four questions indicate that most executive recruiters do not acknowledge encountering the more overt signs of anti-Semitism. However, a sizable minority reports that Jewish applicants for executive positions get less than an equal opportunity. These findings are corroborated by the response to the next question: "Do you find that Jews are less likely than gentiles to get jobs at (a) banks, (b) large industrial companies, or (c) oil companies?"

TABLE III

Do You Find that Jews Are Less Likely than Gentiles to Get Jobs at
(Positive Responses)

City	banks	large industrial companies?	oil companies?
New York	19	12	19
Los Angeles	6	5	4
Philadelphia	2	1	0
TOTAL	27	18	23

It is very significant that 24 per cent of the New York respondents labeled banks as anti-Semitic. Given the close relationships many banks, as well as the oil companies, have with their Arab clients, this is not too surprising.

The figures in Table I indicated that Jews constituted a high percentage of job applicants at many employment agencies, but a relatively low percentage of placements. This meant that Jews were less able to find employment than gentiles. Evidently, Jews still experience more difficulty being placed than gentiles.

When even a substantial minority reports discriminatory employment practices, this is very significant. For reasons we will be discussing, these people have little incentive to acknowledge any form of anti-Semitism, or even to bother returning our questionnaire. When a woman is raped, what are the chances that she will report this to the police? And were someone else to witness a rape or the much less serious crime of discrimination, what are the chances that he would come forth and testify? During a period when it is generally believed that there is no anti-Semitism, it is very significant that these people have testified that they have actually witnessed this phenomenon.

The last item on our questionnaire brings us from the general to the specific: "Could you make a list of ten firms that don't hire Jews or hire very few?" These firms are listed in Table V.

Although it's satisfying to name names, at least two reservations must be noted. The list of firms in Table V cannot be completely accurate. Because executive recruiters in only three cities were queried, many anti-Semitic firms have been left off the list. Others, which have only limited dealing with executive recruiters, have been similarly overlooked. Therefore, the firms in Table V are not the most anti-Semitic corporations, but they are among the most anti-Semitic.

A more serious reservation we had about publishing this list was that it was not only somewhat slanderous, but was assuming guilt before innocence could be established. And yet, these firms were named by at least three executive recruiters. Even in a murder trial one or two witnesses is sufficient to establish guilt.

TABLE IV

JEWS AS A PERCENTAGE OF JOB APPLICANTS AND OF
PLACEMENTS OF EXECUTIVE RECRUITING FIRMS

City	Jews greater % of job applicants than of placements	Jews greater % of placements than of job applicants	Jews same % of job appli- cants as placements
New York	15	8	25
Los Angeles	8	3	7
Philadelphia	4	1	3
TOTAL	27	12	35

TABLE V

FIRMS NAMED BY EXECUTIVE RECRUITERS
HIRING FEW OR NO JEWS[e]

American Arabian Oil
(Aramco) (3)[a]

FMC (3)

IT&T (3)[b]

Johnson & Johnson (4)

Mobil Oil (4)[c]

Westvaco (3)[d]

[a]Numbers in parentheses are the number of executive
recruiters stating that firm hires few or no Jews.

[b]Two executive recruiters stated that IT&T does not
limit its hiring of Jews in most of its divisions
and subsidiaries.

[c]One executive recruiter noted that Mobil limits its
hiring of Jews in all departments except tax and
law. Another, however, said there were Jews in the
personnel department.

[d]One executive recruiter stated that Westvaco, while
still somewhat anti-Semitic, was much more anti-
woman.

[e]Twenty-one companies (not listed here) were each
named by two recruiting firms. At least three of
these, however, hire substantial numbers of Jewish
college graduates, and two others do recruit at
several schools with substantial Jewish enrollments
(See Stephen L. Slavin, "Bias in U.S. Big Business
Recruitment," Patterns of Prejudice, Vol. 10. No. 5,
September-October, 1976.) Rather than name these
and possibly other companies which might be equally
receptive to hiring Jewish applicants, we have named
only those companies which were listed by at least
three executive recruiters.

C. Analysis of Our Survey

Unlike pregnancy, there are varying degrees of anti-Semitic behavior. Any one of the firms on the list might be able to point to its Jewish employees, its published equal opportunity employer policy, or even a Jewish officer or member of the board. Some firms are more anti-Semitic than others, and it is unlikely that any firm on this list can honestly say that (1) a Jew stands the same chance of being hired as a gentile; (2) a Jew stands an equal chance of being promoted; (3) there are reasonable proportions of Jews in middle and upper management positions; and (4) there is a reasonable proportion of Jews in all departments of the company (and not just in computers and sales).

Why don't more executive recruiters acknowledge the extent of anti-Semitism? According to several executive recruiters, one very important factor is whether the recruiter is Jewish or gentile. If he is gentile, he might be simply unaware that Jews aren't being hired. Who notices how many Orientals, Italians or American Indians are being hired (except, of course, when the government calls our attention to its designated minorities)? Why should a gentile take special notice of the number of Jews getting jobs through their agencies?

There is, of course, the possibility that the gentile recruiter is aware of anti-Semitism, but is unwilling to admit it. He himself might be an anti-Semite. But in the words of the Levy's Rye Bread ad, you don't have to be gentile to enjoy anti-Semitism. Some of the best anti-Semites are Jewish. Whether out of self-hatred or because of some less fashionable psychological disorder, there are some Jewish executive recruiters who try to out-WASP the WASP's. As Harry Golden once put it, "The first Jewish President will be an Episcopalian."

Other Jewish executive recruiters might look the other way when dealing with an anti-Semitic corporate personnel representative. When confronted with anti-Semitic behavior, whether the subtle slights of the American establishment, the Eastern European pogroms, or the Final Solution itself, the Jew has usually exhibited a most Christian trait: he turned the other cheek. "If you do anything," they have reasoned, "you'll make it still worse for us." The principal author himself rather leans toward the Old Testament doctrine of an eye for an eye.

Another possible factor was the question of confidentiality. Although we sent a written pledge of anonymity with each questionnaire, some respondents were evidently afraid of losing clients, since most of the questionnaires returned were unsigned. Several told us on the phone that they were concerned with confidentiality. There is no way of telling, however, how many did not reply, or replied that they had no knowledge of anti-Semitism, simply out of fear of reprisal.

Perhaps 20% of the respondents worked with data processing personnel. Many of them noted that while there might be anti-Semitism elsewhere, they were not aware of much, if any, in their own line. One executive recruiter stated that the firms he dealt with were so exacting in their requirements that they would take anyone who met all their qualifications. This gibes with what we have heard elsewhere. Most of the Jews who work for banks seem to be in data processing. For example, at the New York Federal Reserve Bank, this department, unlike any other, is actually dominated by Jews.

Earlier investigations have shown that a large proportion of Jews employed in both the insurance and automobile industries were doing technical work.[7] It seems then, that Jewish employees are sometimes acceptable, provided they keep to themselves. With the phenomenal growth of computers, we may even witness the disappearance of anti-Semitism.

Since the early 1960's, there has been a heightened public consciousness of fair employment legislation. Although most of these laws had been on the books for years, widespread enforcement, and presumably compliance, have been taking place for only the last 15 years. Most firms are very aware of the need to at least appear to be complying with the law, and consequently take care not to make themselves vulnerable to charges of employment discrimination.

Presumably, then, American industry is much less blatantly anti-Semitic than it was in the '50's. This would be reflected by the job orders placed with employment agencies as well as by the observations

of these agencies themselves. Furthermore, since the
agencies are being asked overtly about anti-Semitism,
they are less likely to admit to it, than if they
were simply asked to take anti-Semitic job orders.

D. We All Favor "Our Own Kind."[8]

Several executive recruiters suggested that there
were firms that favored Jewish over gentile applicants.
A few others noted that "Jews preferred Jews and
WASP's preferred WASP's." Some respondents added that
an executive might be more comfortable working with
someone of his own background. Rather than being
motivated by prejudice, he is positively influenced
by the ease with which he is able to relate to someone
who is like himself.

Whether someone gets hired, then, is partically
dependent on his race, sex, religion, and socioeconomic status. WASP's tend to prefer WASP's, Jews
prefer Jews, Blacks favor Blacks, and women tend to
hire other women. That seems like a fair arrangement,
except that if your group is not in a position to
offer you many jobs, your career prospects shrink
considerably. They used to tell poor Black kids --
"in this country there's always the opportunity to work
hard and pull yourself up by your bootstraps." Sure,
but what are the odds against poor Black kids ever
making it? And what are the odds against nice rich
white boys?

We think there's a lot of validity to the
proposition that many firms hire their own kind.
There are so many Jewish firms in heavy industry,
banking, public utilities, and insurance, which
hire most of the nation's college graduates, that the
opportunities for Jewish college graduates are quite
restricted.

Perhaps religion has been superceded by a
more euphemistic selection criterion -- "type."
Is he or she the right type; does this person fit
the company image? One employment agency owner put
it this way: "I might send two equally qualified
applicants to a firm. If the Jewish applicant is
more in the corporate image than his WASP rival, he
is usually hired." And what is the corporate image?
Usually it is a blue-eyed, blond, fairly tall, not
overweight, not too pushy, and not dumb young man.

This does not mean that Jews are not wanted -- indeed an occasional Jew is hired -- it's only the Jewish "type" that is shunned!

The head of an executive search firm in central New Jersey -- not one included in this survey -- told the principal author that she would not bother to send a Jewish applicant for a management position to Johnson & Johnson. "I have to make a living and I won't if I send people who won't get hired." She added that another client from the Midwest had told her -- "I want you to send me someone who'll be compatible. I want a middle-aged WASP male."

Another executive recruiter, Herbert Mines, who appeared with the principal author at an American Jewish Committee colloquim, noted that there was still a certain amount of resistance to hiring Jews for particular positions. His solution? Send Jews for jobs that are open to Jews. He also had to make a living.

Hiring by intangibles has resulted in employment discrimination which government and private efforts are designed to redress. American business, particularly the banks, seek executives who project a certain image -- that image, according to several young Jewish executives is "WASP, tall, blond hair, blue eyes, cleancut, Ivy League, all-American guy." Statistically, we would expect fewer Jews than Protestants to project this image, particularly its first characteristic. As one candid banker (with impeccable "credentials") confided, "Let's face it, Jews can't compete on the 'intangibles.'"

In the wake of the civil rights revolution and the women's liberation movement, corporations have established hiring plans for women, Blacks, Hispanics, and other designated minorities. Perhaps because they have no parallel movement, Jews, who have long suffered as an American minority, have ironically attained the majority stamp without the concomitant rewards.

Jews face a strategic dilemma in trying to make it in the corporate world. Many have attempted, with a certain degree of success, to "pass" as WASP's, while others, either unwilling or unable to go this course, are opting for minority status. This dual strategy undoubtedly obscures the position of American Jews vis-a-vis the Protestant establishment.

"We all feel more at ease with someone who is from the same background," a New York bank Senior Vice President told us. We acknowledged that WASP's tend to prefer WASP's, Jews prefer Jews, Blacks favor Blacks, and women tend to hire other women. That would seem equitable indeed, except that if your group is not in a position to offer many prospects, your career prospects shrink considerably.

Whether or not an employer is motivated by prejudice or simply wanting to be among "his own kind," the results are still the same: Jews are not being hired in major sectors of American industry. Even if we assume that this hiring bias is spread evenly among all groups in our society, the burden falls disproportionately on the Jews, since they are in such a small minority. Until all large corporations hire solely on merit, Jews and other minorities will be at a distinct employment disadvantage.

Chapter Notes

1.   The distinction between an employment agency and an executive search firm is a fine one. In general, employment agencies try to place applicants in whatever positions they can find. Executive search firms, often known as "headhunters," usually are asked by companies to find middle and upper management executives, luring them, if need be, from other firms.

2.   Lois Waldman, "Employment Discrimination Against Jews in the United States -- 1955," Jewish Social Studies, Vol. 18, No. 3, July 1956.

3.   Anti-Defamation League, "Discrimination in Employment," Rights, Vol. 6, No. 1, June 1967, p. 119.

4.   Anti-Defamation League, op. cit., p. 120.

5.   American Jewish Congress (Commission on Law and Social Action), CLSA Reports, (mimeo), March 25, 1955, p. 1.

6.   Jewish anti-Semitism is discussed at length in Chapter IX, Section F.

7.   See Anti-Defamation League, Rights, Vol. 7, No. 1, June 1968, p. 123; Anti-Defamation League, "Detroit's Old Habit," The ADL Bulletin, Vol. 20, No. 9, November 1963, pp. 1 - 2.

8.   Parts of this section appeared in our article, "The Corporate WASP," which appeared in the Summer, 1979, issue of The Jewish Spectator.

CHAPTER VII

SURVEY OF COLLEGE ALUMNI PUBLICATIONS

A. Introduction

We have been looking at corporate recruitment and
hiring patterns from several vantage points. Chapter
IV and V examined corporate recruitment patterns,
while in the preceding chapter we observed executive
recruitment through employment agencies. Now we
shall use alumni newsletters and directories from some
of our 170 colleges to provide us with still more
data on corporate employment.

Letters were sent to the alumni organizations of
the 170 colleges (see Section A of the Appendix for
a listing of these colleges) in September, 1975.
We asked for copies of the two or three most recent
alumni newletters, which often listed the jobs
currently held by some of the graduates. After
follow-up letters were sent, we received usable data
from 67 schools.

Several of these schools also published alumni
directories listing the positions held by most of
the graduates. By January, 1976, ten colleges sent
copies of their directories, from each of which we
took a sample of 2,000 alumni jobs. The data from
these publications and from the newsletters provide
us with some very discernable corporate employment
patterns with regard to Jews and gentiles.

B.   The Data

     In Chapter IV we divided corporations into six
categories -- the top 100 industrial companies, the
next 400, insurance companies, banks, the top 50
public utilities, and other public utilities. The
same format is used in each of the following tables.
As in the preceding two chapters, we distinguish
between Jewish and gentile names. In every table
we are making a comparison of the employment patterns
of Jews and gentiles.

     In Table I we compare the employment of alumni
from schools with low Jewish enrollments with that
of alumni from schools with high Jewish enrollments.
As the figures in this table clearly indicate, alumni
from schools with low Jewish enrollments have averaged
higher corporate employment than alumni from the more
predominantly Jewish schools. This pattern is
repeated in each of the six employment categories
under consideration.

     The data for Table I were drawn from the alumni
newsletters of 67 colleges, 53 of which had low
Jewish enrollments and 14 of which had high Jewish
enrollments. For example, one can easily observe
that an average of 12.7 alumni from the schools of
low Jewish enrollment were employed at the top 100
industrial firms, whereas an average of only 6.6
alumni from the predominantly Jewish schools were so
employed.

     And yet, the figures shown in Table I grossly
underestimate the dichotomy between Jewish and non-
Jewish employment. Two additional factors need to
be taken into account. Although most of the schools
with high Jewish enrollment were always predominantly
Jewish, there are some which have only recently
begun accepting high numbers of Jewish applicants.
Most notable among these are Wesleyan, Yale and the

110

TABLE I

CORPORATE EMPLOYMENT OF COLLEGE ALUMNI
1974-1975

Average number of alumni from colleges with
low Jewish enrollments[a]

Fortune's[b] top industrial firms		Insurance Companies	Banks	Fortune's top 50 Public Utilities	Other Public Utilities
top 100	next 400				
12.7	8.7	5.9	12.9	0.9	1.0

Average number of alumni from colleges with
high Jewish enrollments[c]

6.6	6.5	5.6	11.1	0.2	0.4

[a]Less than 30% of the undergraduate enrollment are Jews.

[b]Each year <u>Fortune</u> magazine publishes a list of the nation's top industrial firms, banks, insurance companies and public utilities. These firms are ranked by sales.

[c]At least 30% of the undergraduate enrollment is Jewish.

Source: Alumni newsletters from 67 colleges

University of Pennslyvania. Penn, whose undergraduate
enrollment is now 40% Jewish, was, until recent years,
a predominantly WASP institution. Since the employment
data obtained from the University of Pennsylvania
alumni newsletters consists of the positions held by
alumni who graduated over the last 40 years, many of
these positions are associated with student bodies
that were considerably less than 40% Jewish.

If we are correct that gentiles are more easily
hired than Jews, then the alumni employment figures
of schools with rising Jewish enrollments are upwardly
biased. But a much more potent factor is that within
the heavily Jewish schools, it is usually the gentile
alumnus who finds corporate employment. Both of these
factors inflate the employment averages of the
predominantly Jewish schools shown in Table I. By
name analysis, however, these figures can be deflated
to render a more accurate picture of the true employment patterns of Jewish and gentile graduates.[1]

We have modified the figures of Table I by
eliminating two classes of employed alumni data:
(1) Jews from schools with low Jewish enrollments,
and (2) gentiles from schools with high Jewish
enrollments. The effect of these changes is to enable
us to compare the employment of non-Jews from
predominantly gentile schools with that of Jews from
schools with high Jewish enrollments. These modified
figures are shown in Table II.

One will notice that nearly all the figures
in Table II are lower than their counterparts in
Table I. In the upper parts of both tables, the
changes are relatively small since there were very
few Jews listed in the alumni newsletters of the
predominantly gentile schools. However, at the schools
with high Jewish enrollments, most of the corporate
positions held by alumni are held by gentiles. This
finding is rather significant and we shall be returning
to it toward the end of this chapter.

Table II presents a striking contrast between the
average number of positions held by Jewish and gentile
alumni in each of the six categories of company
considered. In every case, the gentile average is
over three times the Jewish average, but the averages
for Jews and gentiles employed by industrial companies
and banks are particularly noteworthy. As we turn
now to the employment data from the alumni directories,
we will come across very similar findings.

112

TABLE II

CORPORATE EMPLOYMENT OF COLLEGE ALUMNI:
A MODIFICATION[d]
1074-1975

Average number of alumni from colleges with
low Jewish enrollments[a]

Fortune's[b] top industrial firms		Insurance Companies	Banks	Fortune's top 50 Public Utilities	Other Public Utilities
top 100	next 400				
12.5	8.6	5.5	11.9	0.9	1.0

Average number of alumni from colleges with
high Jewish enrollments[c]

1.5	1.8	1.4	2.0	0.1	0.0

notes a, b, and c: See corresponding notes in Table I.

[d] Only gentile alumni are included in the average
number of alumni from colleges with low Jewish
enrollments. Only Jewish alumni are included in
the average number of alumni from colleges with
high Jewish enrollments. Thus, Jewish alumni from
predominantly gentile schools and gentile alumni
from predominantly Jewish schools have been eliminated from consideration. This elimination is
reflected in a comparison of the figures in Table
II with those in Table I.

Source: Alumni newsletters from 67 colleges

Because there are only ten schools with alumni
directories listing positions held by graduates, it
is possible to list these schools separately in
Tables II and V. These will again provide employment
averages, by company category. Table III is an interschool comparison of averages, while Table V provides
intra-school comparisons of the employment of Jews
and gentiles. Tables IV and VI are composites of the
data from the tables which precede them.

The schools in Table III are listed in order of
increasing Jewish enrollment, beginning with Clemson,
only 0.5% of whose student body is Jewish and ending
with Baruch, with a student body that is 47.5% Jewish.
We have been using a 30% level as the dividing line
between heavily Jewish and predominantly non-Jewish
schools, so evidently only Wesleyan and Baruch represent the heavily Jewish schools. Very few schools
print alumni directories, so Harvard Business School
and Wharton (University of Pennsylvania) are included
in this survey.

Table III shows the number of positions held
by the graduates of the ten colleges which published
alumni directories. A sample of 2,000 names was
taken from each directory. From each sample it was
determined how many graduates held positions in any
of our six corporate categories. By name analysis,
we decided which of these people were Jewish.

Using Gettysburg as an example, we can see that
of the 2,000 alumni sampled, 136 worked for the top
100 industrial firms, 72 worked for one of the 400
next largest industrial firms, 83 were with banks,
57 with insurance companies and 14 held positions
with the top 50 public utilities. The number of
Jewish alumni employed by each of these types of
firms is indicated by the figures in parentheses.

In the cases of the schools with extremely low
Jewish enrollments, Clemson, Gettysburg, and perhaps,
Alfred, one would not expect to find very many Jewish
graduates listing jobs in their alumni directories.
However, if we look at the schools with higher Jewish
enrollments, we find in each case that Jews are
markedly underrepresented in terms of positions held.
Starting with Franklin & Marshall, although the
student body is 22% Jewish, we find that in no case
do Jews hold 22% of the positions in any of the six
company categories. Among positions held by Harvard
Business School graduates, only insurance companies

114

TABLE III

CORPORATE EMPLOYMENT OF COLLEGE ALUMNI, BY COLLEGE[a] 1973-1975[b]

Total number of alumni listing positions, from colleges with varying Jewish enrollments

College & Jewish percentage share of enrollment	Fortune's[c] top industrial firms		Insurance Companies	Banks	Fortune's top 50 Public Utilities	Other Public Utilities
	top 100	next 400[d]				
Clemson (0.5%)	163	147 (1)	25	32	31	23
Gettysburgh (2.7%)	136 (7)	72 (2)	83 (2)	57 (1)	14 (1)	0
Alfred (7.8%)	227 (6)	207 (6)	34 (2)	39 (2)	1	7
Tufts (10.0%)	216 (16)	79 (2)	45 (5)	28 (2)	7	9
Georgetown (12.4%)	98 (5)	42 (1)	46 (1)	90 (1)	7	1
Franklin & Marshall (22.0%)	87 (7)	55 (4)	33 (4)	61 (4)	3	0
Harvard Business School (25.0%)	334 (17)	161 (15)	37 (16)	169 (6)	19	0
Wharton (28.1%)[e]	121 (6)	94 (5)	37 (8)	246 (17)	14 (2)	0
Wesleyan (33.0%)	185 (12)	81 (5)	128 (4)	124 (2)	4 (1)	2
Baruch (47.5%)	78 (26)	48 (18)	32 (13)	65 (19)	8 (2)	0

TABLE III -- Continued

[a]A sample of 2,000 names was taken from each alumni
directory. The numbers in the body of this table
are the numbers of alumni who listed positions in
each of the six categories of corporation. The
numbers in parentheses are the Jewish alumni in these
positions.

[b]These ten colleges were among the very few which
put out alumni directories; they are seldom published
more than once every few years. The directories
from which this data was complied were the most
up-to-date available.

[c]See footnote b of Table I.

[d]Numbers in parentheses denote employment of Jewish
alumni and are included in figures to their
immediate left.

[e]The undergraduate enrollment at the University of
Pennsylvania is 40% Jewish. Although the graduate
percentage share of Jews at Wharton is somewhat
lower, no figures are available. My own sample
of 28.1% is possibly a little on the low side.

Source: Alumni directories of each of the colleges
listed.

employees are more than 25% Jewish. And even more
interestingly, in no case do Jewish graduates of
Wesleyan or Baruch hold corporate jobs in proportion
to their percentage of undergraduate enrollment.

Let us turn now to Table IV, which gives a composite view of the data presented in the preceding
table. To provide a basis of comparison between
schools with high and low Jewish enrollments (using
30% as the dividing line), we have calculated the
average number of alumni working for each of the
six types of corporations. By adding, for example,
the number of alumni of the seven schools with low
Jewish enrollments employed by the top 100 industrial
firms (163 + 136 ... = 1381) and dividing that sum
by 8, we get 172.6. This number is then compared
to the average for Wesleyan and Baruch (185 + 78 =
263/2 = 131.5), 131.5.

These comparisons apparently show very mixed
results. The predominantly Jewish schools, Wesleyan
and Baruch lead substantially in jobs at insurance
companies and marginally in bank jobs, while the
predominantly gentile schools hold large leads in the
four other corporate categories.

These differences can easily be resolved, however,
if we turn back again to Wesleyan's banking and
insurance company figures in Table III. Of the 128
insurance jobs held by Wesleyan graduates, only four
were held by Jews. Similarly, only 2 of the 124
alumni at banks were Jewish. It is clear, then,
that Wesleyan's gentile alumni accounted for the
high averages for bank and insurance company jobs.

To a lesser degree, this observation also holds
true for Baruch's graduates. One might further note
the possibility of various qualitative differences
in the types of jobs held by Jews and gentiles. It
had been observed by the Anti-Defamation League
that Jews were often relegated to sales jobs at
insurance companies, rather than to the more numerous
inside jobs.[2] Of the 13 Jewish graduates from Baruch
who work for insurance companies, seven are salesmen.
And yet, only one of the 19 gentiles is in sales.

Until now we have made only interschool
comparisons to determine if there were significant
differences between the number of jobs held by the
alumni of predominantly Jewish and gentile schools.
We shall now address ourselves to the key question

117

TABLE IV

CORPORATE EMPLOYMENT OF COLLEGE ALUMNI: A COMPOSITE
1973-1975

Average number of alumni listing positions: from
colleges with low Jewish enrollments[a]

Fortune's[b] top industrial firms		Insurance Companies	Banks	Fortune's top 50 Public Utilities	Other Public Utilities
top 100	next 400				
172.6[d]	107.1	42.5	92.5	12.0	5.0

Average number of alumni listing positions: from
colleges with high Jewish enrollments[c]

| 131.5 | 64.5 | 80 | 94.5 | 6 | 1 |

[a]Less than 30% of the undergraduate enrollment are
Jews; included here is Harvard Business School whose
enrollment, like the undergraduate school, is 25%
Jewish.

[b]See footnote b of Table I.

[c]At least 30% of the undergraduate enrollment is
Jewish.

[d]These averages are obtained by adding the employment
figures for each corporate category in Table III and
dividing that sum by seven for the colleges with low
Jewish enrollments and by two for the colleges with
high Jewish enrollments.

Source: See Table III.

in this chapter -- the distribution of jobs among the
alumni of each school. To do this we have taken a
sample of 250 Jewish and gentile graduates from each
alumni directory.[3]

C. Analysis of the Data

     Even a cursory examination of the data in Table V
would reveal a striking pattern between the Jewish and
gentile alumni of each college: the gentiles have
an overwhelming superiority in terms of jobs with
large corporations. In almost every instance, jobs
held by gentiles are two, three, or even eight or
nine times as numerous as those held by Jews. Of
the 45 matched set of data (nine schools, five corporate categories each) in only two instances do Jewish-
held jobs exceed those held by gentiles.

     When we view these data as aggregates (see Table
VI), the Jewish-gentile dichotomy takes on added
significance. The employment of gentiles is about
three times that for Jews for every type of firm.
When we put this finding together with our earlier
data on interschool comparisons (Tables I and II),
we should reach two inescapable conclusions: (1)
alumni from schools with low Jewish enrollments are
more often hired than those from schools with high
Jewish enrollments; and (2) gentile graduates are
more often hired than Jewish graduates from the same
college.

     But even now we are not quite finished! The
corporate employment picture for Jewish college
graduates would be still more stark if we were to
eliminate a small group of relatively open firms. By
these we mean the companies that apparently have been
hiring people without undue regard to race, religion,
and perhaps "type" (often corporations prefer blue-eyed,
blond-haired, WASP males).

     Table VII is a list of these firms and of the
number of Jewish alumni from our sample employed with
each. Although the numbers are small, they add up to
be a substantial percentage of the total number of
Jewish college graduates who work for large corporations. It is also interesting that four of these
firms -- Burlington Industries, the New York Times,
Norton Simon, and RCA -- are owned by Jews.

TABLE V

CORPORATE EMPLOYMENT OF JEWISH AND GENTILE GRADUATES OF EIGHT COLLEGES[a]
1973-1975[b]

Number of alumni listing positions

College	Fortune's top industrial firms		Insurance Companies	Banks	Public Utilities[d]
	top 100	next 400			
Gettysburg					
Jews	7	2	2	1	1
Gentiles	12	27	12	3	2
Alfred					
Jews	6	6	2	2	0
Gentiles	24	16	3	1	0
Tufts					
Jews	16	2	5	2	0
Gentiles	32	17	8	5	3
Georgetown					
Jews	10	7	4	3	0
Gentiles	18	9	15	3	0
Franklin & Marshall					
Jews	3	3	1	3	0
Gentiles	15	11	4	7	1
Harvard Business School					
Jews	9	7	0	3	1
Gentiles	30	18	3	27	1
Wharton					
Jews	2	4	4	6	1
Gentiles	26	16	3	40	1

TABLE V -- Continued

Number of alumni listing positions

Colleges	Fortune's top industrial firms		Insurance Companies	Banks	Public Utilities[d]
	top 100	next 400			
Wesleyan					
Jews	13	4	7	2	2
Gentiles	25	13	14	15	5
Baruch					
Jews	3	8	1	3	0
Gentiles	27	19	7	18	2

[a] Clemson is not included because 250 identifiable Jewish names could not be found in the directly.

[b] See footnote b of Table III.

[c] See footnote b of Table I.

[d] Due to the small numbers of individuals involved, all public utility employment is included here under one heading.

Source: Alumni directories of each of the colleges listed.

TABLE VI

CORPORATE EMPLOYMENT OF JEWISH AND GENTILE GRADUATES
OF NINE COLLEGES: A COMPOSITE[a]
1973-1975[b]

Number of alumni listing positions

Alumni	Fortune's[c] top industrial firms top 100	next 400	Insurance Companies	Banks	Public Utilities[d]
Jews	69	43	26	25	5
Gentiles	183	130	66	79	14

notes a - d: See corresponding notes of Table V.

Source: See Table V.

TABLE VII

LARGE INDUSTRIAL FIRMS EMPLOYING TWO OR
MORE JEWISH ALUMNI
1973-1975

Fortune's Top Industrial Firms	Number of Jews Employed
Top 100:	
Burlington Industries	3
DuPont	3
General Electric	3
IBM	12
IT&T	3
Raytheon	2
RCA	12
United Aircraft	3
Xerox	3
	44
Next 400:	
Hercules	2
N.Y. Times	2
Norton Simon	2
Colt Industries	2
	8

Source: See Table III.

There are 52 Jews employed by these firms -- 44 by the top 100 and 8 by the next 400. From Table VI we see that there were only 69 Jews at the top 100 industrial firms and 43 at the next 400. This means that this handful of firms employed 63.8% of the Jews working for the top 100 and 18.6% of those with the next 400. If we put these figures together, we find that of the 112 Jewish alumni employed by Fortune's top 500 industrial firms, 52, or 46.4%, are employed by only 13, or 2.6%, of all the firms. And just two of the companies, IBM and RCA account for 24 (21.4%) of all the Jewish employees.

Since it is obvious that considerably less than proportionate numbers of Jewish graduates have been hired by large corporations, we must reconsider our earlier findings. Not only have these companies avoided Jewish colleges, but they have avoided Jewish students during their rare visits. This means that we really have two levels of avoidance, both of which we are able to measure indirectly.

Not only are heavily Jewish schools avoided, but even when these schools are visited, the Jewish graduates are somehow screened out. By hindsight, then, we can say that the data in Chapter IV really understated the degree of corporate anti-Semitism. And apparently, this understatement was quite substantial. However, this isn't entirely unexpected: if corporate recruiters avoid Jewish schools, then they would be consistent in discouraging or avoiding Jewish applicants.

Chapter Notes

1. There are many "typically" Jewish and gentile names. The basis of differentiation between these types of names is fully explained in Appendix C.

2. Anti-Defamation League, Rights, Vol. 7, No. 1, June 1968, p. 123. See also, Rights, Vol. 2, No. 8, November-December, 1959, pp. 59 - 61.

3. Clemson is not included in this sampling because we could not find 250 identifiable Jewish names in the directory.

CHAPTER VIII

ANTI-SEMITISM AT THE LARGE NEW YORK BANKS[1]

> They own, you know the banks in the
> country, the newspapers. Just look
> at where the Jewish money is.
>
>> General George S. Brown
>> Chairman, Joint Chiefs of
>> Staff.

> Bankers obey the law.
>
>> William Eiseman
>> Director of Personnel
>> Morgan Guaranty

A. Do the Jews Own the Banks -- or Even Work for Them?

Do the Jews own the banks? What is the position of Jews in the major banks in New York, the financial center of the country?

Quinley and Glock report that according to a 1975 Harris poll 14 per cent of Americans

> ...saw Jews as controlling "big New York banks," but 30 per cent in addition saw them as playing an "important role." In another section of the same survey, respondents were asked whether they agreed with a recent statement by General Brown that Jews 'own the banks and newspapers in this country.' Twenty per cent replied in the affirmative.[2]

Discrimination against Jews persists in the hiring patterns at two of New York's seven leading banks. Morgan and Irving Trust are the banks singled out for their apparent reluctance to hire qualified Jews, reveals a recent study by the Civil Rights Division of the New York Attorney General's office. These findings are based on a survey of 1000 June 1977 MBA graduates of Columbia and New York University. The attorney General's study, as well as the authors' independent research, provide new evidence that Jews are still virtually excluded from bank management.

In this chapter we'll examine in some depth this little-known anomaly of the age of equal opportunity. Along the way we'll try to resolve some widespread misconceptions about Jews in banking.

The major problem, of course, is determining who is Jewish. Using Standard & Poor's corporate register, we first sought to identify Jewish executives by surname. We contacted all officers with "obviously" or possibly Jewish names to verify their

TABLE I

Bank	Top Executive Officers *		Senior Management **		Senior Officers ***	
	Jews	All	Jews	All	Jews	All
Bankers Trust	0	2	2	14	4	44
Chase	0	3	0	18	1	74
Chemical	0	3	1	10	6	51
Citibank	0	4	0	14	2	64
Irving Trust	0	2	0	9	1	27
Manufacturers	0	3	0	8	1	44
Morgan	0	5	0	13	1	41
	0	22	3	86	16	345

*   Also on Board of Directors

**   Includes President, Board Chairman, Vice Chairman and Executive Vice Presidents

*** All officers from Chairman to Senior Vice President

religious identification. Some people with such
apparently Jewish names as Levey, Marks, and Schwartz
in fact turned out to be gentiles. (See Appendix.)

We consulted bank personnel officers but they
usually professed no knowledge of their colleagues'
religious backgrounds. When, however, we had ferreted
out the few Jewish officers, they seeemed to have a
pretty good idea of who else was Jewish and who wasn't.
We believe we have accounted for every senior officer
who considers him/herself to be Jewish. Like the
United Jewish Appeal, we didn't leave a Cohen unturned.

There is not one Jew among the twenty-two officers who are also directors in New York's major banks.
Only three of the top eighty-six officers (executive
vice preisdent and up) are Jewish; that's 3.5 per cent.
When we consider 345 senior officers (including senior
vide presidents), there is a grand total of sixteen
Jews, or 4.6 per cent. In other words, our detailed
survey doesn't bear out General Brown's more im-
pressionistic assessment.

B. But Why?

Three main explanations are advanced about why
Jews are so underrepresented in the upper echelons
of bank management. A first rationale is that today's
managers, who began their careers twenty or thirty
years ago, reflect the hiring patterns of the '40's
and '50's.

Many would concede anti-Semitism in banking that
long ago. The ready explanation was that Jews were
just too ambitious to work for the low starting sala-
ries the banks were then paying. In addition, Jews
tend to get the very technical and specialized staff
positions in banks -- computer programming, law, or
public relations -- and these don't afford upward
mobility in bank management.

A third explanation was expressed by a high-
ranking Jewish officer: "None of us could ever get
to be President or Chairman because we can't get
experience with the large customers." Several others
echoed the sentiment that national and international
lending experience are requisite credentials for top
bank officers, yet Jews are often steered away from

these areas. A young officer at Manufacturers Hanover told us that "Those [Jews] who do get into national lending are usually discouraged by their superiors' not promoting them."

We might note in passing that Jews are considered too ambitious to work for banks, but when they do, they seem to be in areas of limited advancement potential. Surely few Jews have pushed their way into national and international lending.

Are there so few Jews at the New York banks because the banks won't hire very many, or is that Jews don't apply? Several highly-placed officers (both Jewish and gentile) at various large New York banks believe that not many Jews apply for bank jobs. Successful Jewish bankers like Alan Fishman, a senior v.p. at Chemical, say that "banking offers excellent opportunities for anyone with motivation and ability."

Certainly there are individual examples of successful Jewish officers at each of the large New York banks. But are they tokens, or do their examples truly indicate a wide-open field with merit the only criterion for success? And next year in Jerusalem?

C. Management Trainees

Are the New York banks, in recruiting tomorrow's top managers, now compensating for the long-standing absence of Jews? Over the past decade, several of the banks have taken on an increasing number of Jewish officer trainees. Most of them have been drawn from the ranks of M.B.A.s graduating from various schools around the country. To appraise the current trend toward hiring Jewish officers, we took a close look at the job offers made to the graduates of Columbia and New York University business schools, each of which is about one-third Jewish.

In a survey of 1,000 June 1977 graduates of Columbia and N.Y.U., the Civil Rights Division of the New York State Attorney General's office sent each a questionnaire listing the major New York banks and asking them to note which, if any, had made job offers. About 25 per cent of the graduates responded. The results were tabulated to determine

if there were any disriminatory hiring patterns with
respect to religion. These results are summarized
in Table II.

What is most striking here is that two banks did
not find even one qualified Jewish applicant. Yet
between them they found thirteen Catholics and
Protestants who met their standards. Each of the
other five large New York banks made job offers to
at least two Jews.

In two groups of recently-accepted trainees at
Morgan, a grand total of three Jews were among the 67
hired. When we consider that Morgan (as well as the
other New York banks) does nearly all its hiring from
out-of-town schools, with relatively low Jewish enrollments, it becomes more evident why banking is in
no immediate danger of being overrun by Jews.

D.   Banks that are "Good" for the Jews

In terms of absolute numbers, Jews seem to fare
best at Bankers Trust, Chemical, and Manufacturers-
Hanover. Bob Russell, v.p. in charge of personnel
at Bankers Trust, reported to us that as of July
1975, 173 of 1800 officers were Jewish (9.3%). At
Chemical , according to one internal source, about
150 officers, or about 10%, are Jewish. At Manufacturers-Hanover some 126 of 2445 officers (5.2%)
were Jewish at the time of the Attorney General's
previous survey (dated January 10, 1968). Both
Jewish and gentile officers told us that now about
10% of the bank's officers are Jewish.

These are the banks that are "good for the Jews,"
and they have, at best, 10% management-level Jews:
This in a city where half the college graduates
are Jewish? Many thousands of Jews who majored in
business, accounting, and economics have been
graduated from the City University each of the last
four decades. Yet only a handful to date have become
officers in the city's seven biggest banks.

To help get a management trainee job at Manufacturers-Hanover, it helps to know a high-ranking
officer. Many of the management trainees are sons
of out-of-town, well-to-do, businessmen, who have
long done business with local banks. These banks

TABLE II

Bank	Catholics		Jews		Protestants	
	Applications	Job offers	Applications	Job offers	Applications	Job offers
Bankers Trust	29	4	25	5	24	3
Chase	28	7	26	5	24	4
Chemical	27	3	25	5	22	4
Citibank	40	9	28	8	38	10
Irving Trust	22	4	24	0	23	4
Manufacturers	18	1	17	2	13	3
Morgan	25	2	18	0	23	3
TOTAL	189	30	163	25	167	31

have correspondent relationships with Manufacturers-Hanover and provide entree for the well-connected youth. Similar arrangements are made for well-connected provincials at the other large New York banks as well.

After putting in five or six years at the New York bank and attaining the vice presidential title, the young man leaves New York to return to his home town. He can either work for his father or become a top officer at the local bank. Or, of course, he is welcome to stay at the big bank.

Where does this leave the Jewish applicant? Usually out in the cold. There are, of course, instances of well-connected Jewish boys with "ins" at one of the New York banks, but they are rare exceptions.

At the end of the management training period, usually two or three years, there is a choice of going into metropolitan, national, or international lending. A lending officer must be able to relate on a personal level with his corporate counterpart. Personal contacts in the corporate world are helpful here. Since there are relatively few Jewish firms among the Fortune 500, Jewish management trainees are not encouraged to go into national lending. Since it is this area that provides the fastest management track, the low numbers of Jews at the bottom explains their absence at the top.

Like New York's other leading banks, Manufacturers-Hanover's Jewish officers are concentrated in "Jewish jobs" -- factoring, legal work, computer programming, and the like. The top-ranking Jewish officer is in the metropolitan area. His area includes the garment district.

Moving along to Chase and Citibank, we find considerably lower percentages of Jewish officers. In mid-1969, an Attorney General's report listed Chase as having 43 Jewish officers out of 2,763, while Citibank had 103 out of 3,444. It is the consensus of officers (Jewish and gentile) we spoke with that the percentage share of Jews at both banks has risen to about 5%.

E.   The "Bankers Banks"

Finally we come to those venerable "bankers'
banks," Morgan Guaranty and Irving Trust. Consistently
officers at each of the seven banks have singled out
these two as having a reputation for anti-Semitism.
An Attorney General's Report dated June 10, 1969,
stated that at that time there were only 11 Jewish
officers out of the 447 at Irving. In eight years
this number has increased slightly. At present, of
206 v.p.s, eight or nine are Jewish, but none is at
or near the top. One of them told us: "There is an
informal quota system at Irving: Don't hire more than
a small percentage of Jews; if 30 slots are open, hire
maybe one or two."

Morgan presented the starkest picture. John M.
Keyes, then v.p. in charge of personnel for the bank,
was quoted in the same memo of the Artorney General's
office: "I believe we do have a few Jewish officers,
five or six officers are unhesitatingly Jewish."
Whatever that means. Paul Luftig, formerly the
President of Franklin National, told the authors
that there probably were a few "hidden" Jewish
officers at Morgan. We leave it to the reader to
reflect upon why some Jews would be "unhesitatingly
Jewish," while others would choose to remain "hidden."

At the time of the 1969 report Morgan had 792
officers, about 10 of whom were thought to be Jewish.
At the present time Morgan has over 900 officers based
in New York, and estimates of the number of Jewish
officers now vary from under 20 to "well over 30." The
highest estimate is that of William Eiseman, senior vice
president in charge of personnel. Thirteen years ago
the Attorney General's office had this to say about
Morgan: "One can only conclude that Morgan has not,
in the past, made a good faith effort to provide
executive opportunities to all qualified applicants
regardless of race, creed, or color." Nothing has
changed: Instead there's evidence that Jews are
still not welcome at the bank.

The few Jewish officers who do work at Morgan are
concentrated in (non-banking) staff or operations jobs.
We located two in the legal department, two in economic and corporate research, five or six in methods
and systems, and one or two in manpower development.
But no one has identified for us any national or

135

or international lending officer who is "unhesitatingly" Jewish.

Why, then, does Morgan have so few Jewish officers, particularly in the lending area? The frequent explanation is that Morgan, as a wholesale bank , does very little business with Jews. A Chase or a Citibank does a great deal of local (i.e., Jewish) business as well as national business. Since it is human nature for people to want to do business with others like themselves, banks try to accommodate their customers. This is pandering to the presumed prejudice of the customers, even if it did not show anti-Semitism within the bank's management.

Other bankers have mentioned a related rationale. What we have here is a club. As Luftig noted, "If the guy from American Can is a Yale man, your guy should be. You can send a Jewish loan officer to Jonathan Logan, but not to Boeing. This is not because of anti-Semitism on the part of the borrower, but because the banks are somewhat retrogressive."

A highly-placed officer at Morgan explained that many of the men at his bank have traditionally been socialites. These people move only in very restricted social circles, frequent clubs that still virtually exclude Jews. There is a very clear preference for the "WASP-type." Another Morgan officer speculated that those responsible for hiring "tended to be most receptive toward people who were most like themselves -- conservative , WASP, graduates of prestigious private colleges, and from relatively affluent backgrounds."

It is interesting that the officers we interviewed at Morgan -- Jewish as well as gentile -- pretty much fit this description. Apparently Morgan will hire anyone -- Black, Hispanic, Jewish, or whatever -- so long as he looks like a WASP. We were told that when Morgan hired its first black officer , hundreds of people got off the elevator (even though it wasn't their floor) to get a look at this man. Evidently he was an extraordinary physical specimen -- the first Black to pass the Morgan WASP Test!

The ideal Morgan officer, one Morgan v.p. told us, should "...project a sense of conservatism, or maybe a better word is confidence , because we are obviously the protectors of one's monies and in our business impressions are terribly important.... It was very difficult for Jews to be in that image. They weren't in that image, but more in the image of Seventh Avenue."

Maybe the real reason there are so few Jews in banking, and particularly lending, is this predilection for a pinstriped Protestant. It goes without saying that banks cultivate a conservative image of solidity their borrowers find reassuring. Bankers dress understatedly, are impeccably groomed, and tend to blandness.

Furthermore, banks tend to shrink from controversy -- anything that focuses attention to them, especially if it might alienate or antagonize their customers. Bankers perceive their customers as conservative and perhaps make assumptions about their prejudices. Bankers Trust has sent a few Black loan officers to the South and we know of a few occasions of banks sending a Jew to a supposedly anti-Semitic customer. These have been, however, exceptions to the rule: Don't make waves.

F. Old-Boy Network[3]

What happens when the Jew, a perennial outsider, tries for an "insider" job in banking. A Jewish officer at Chase Manhattan described the role of Jews at his bank. "Sometimes they use our brains. But the guys who run the bank is an 'Old-Boy' system. If there is an open job, they hire a nice gentile boy with a good 'background.' They may be very personable young fellows, but you can't run a bank like a fraternity. The Old-Boy system is good until the bank suffers losses. I've sensed a staleness and lack of efficiency around Chase. You know what's happened to this bank in the last few years." Chase, long Number 1 in American banking, has slipped to Number 3.

One disgruntled Jewish bank officer told us, "Jews can work in banks -- as long as they don't get too close to the money." An indication of how Jews are treated is the allocation of jobs within the large New York banks. One officer at Irving Trust told us that Italians and Jews have traditionally been confined to operations rather than lending at

most banks. Of the 50-odd Jewish bank officers we
interviewed, all but three were either in computer
programming, accounting, public relations, legal
work, economic analysis, personnel, real estate
operations, or factoring. At Chase and Citibank,
with extensive computer opations, in some sections
over half the programmers are Jewish. Even at
Morgan, the top two legal slots are filled by Jews.
We can almost discount the role of these officers,
since they are so peripheral to the real business
of banking.

G. The Jews who are There

How did the Jews who are there get into banking?
Many got in through factoring. The major New York
banks have acquired most of the independent factoring
houses, which, traditionally, catered to the textile
and garment industries.

The major New York banks "acquired," rather
than hired, many of their Jewish officers. Chemical
still has officers from Dommerreich Factors, Citibank
from Hubsman Factors, and Bankers Trust from Coleman
Factors and Public National Bank. Chase has acquired
Shapiro Factors and over a dozen Jewish officers are
still on board.

The Jews, then, who came into banking through
the back door of factoring, were not even hired by
their present employers, the big New York banks. Since
their work is specialized and only tenuously connected
with banking, they can scarcely be seen as a cabal
of Jewish bankers. Louis Moskowitz, who had owned
Dommerreich Factors, became a senior v.p. with
Chemical, but his case is virtually unique. A few
years ago he moved on to Republic National as an
executive v.p. One of his friends at another large
New York bank even remarked to us, "Louie isn't a
banker!" Once a factorer, always a factorer.

Traditionally banking is divided into two main
activities -- operations and lending. Operations
involves computer programming, clerical work, check
processing, and personnel work. An operations officer
at Citibank observed, "Operations officers are mostly
Jewish and Italian, while lending officers tend to
be Ivy League WASPs." The reason that a high proportion

of Jewish bank officers end up in nonbanking positions
is discriminatory promotion practices. Jews tend to
go into technical and professional areas where merit
is rewarded. Most would agree that in corporate
lending, where promotions could be based on more sub-
jective criteria, there are very few Jews. According
to several Jews in middle management at Citibank and
Chase, those Jews who do work there are often hired for
their specialized training. Loan officers, however,
are given on-the-job training.

H.   Jews in the Era of Equal Opportunity

Because of the real or imagined customer preferences, banks do not hire Jews for visible, client-
contact positions in the lending end of banking. We
don't know whether the banks' hiring patterns reflect
anti-Semitism or merely a pragmatic accommodation to
reality. We do know that Jews are being turned away
solely because they are Jewish. And this is illegal.

While Blacks and women appear finally to be
making significant vocational strides, Jews continue
to be bypassed in banking. We've been given several
explanations, none completely satisfactory:

● The government now treats Jews as part of the
white majority, who presumably need no hiring quotas
or other special protection.

● Jews are less likely to be aware of employment
discrimination than other minority groups. For
example, who really notices how many Jews work at
a particular bank (besides the authors?) Blacks
and women, obviously, are more readily identifiable.

● Jews are not inclined to make waves; 2,000 years
of persecution will tend to have that effect.

● Prejudice against Jews is, in the world of banking, subtle. Several Jewish officers told us that
they felt vaguely uncomfortable at their banks, yet
they rarely heard any overtly anti-Semitic comments,
at least on upper managerial levels. A Jew can never
be sure why he wasn't hired or promoted.

We have tried to show statistically how banks
still discriminate against Jews. We have located a

few highly-placed Jews at each of the seven leading New York banks. However, all seven essentially remain WASP preserves. Findings of the Attorney General's office and our own research indicate that qualified Jewish applicants are not getting jobs in banking comparable to other business school graduates. When one Jew is turned down by various banks, this proves very little, but when a pervasive pattern of avoidance towards Jews emerges, it becomes clear that anti-Semitism is still alive and well in some New York banks.

Not everything is good for the Jews, today, in the New York banking community. In fairness, we must note that the situation was worse ten or fifteen years ago. Many bankers, Jewish and gentile, have perceived a marked decline in anti-Semitism over the last decade. Not long ago it would have been difficult to imagine that Chase would have a kosher cafeteria or that Bankers Trust would print a Jewish calendar.

But will there ever be a Jewish president of a major New York bank? Paul Luftig believes that day will not come until Jews are permiited to acquire lending experience. A Jewish v.p. at Chase put it this way: "I doubt if we'll see anti-Semitism in banking eliminated in our time."

What happens now? Thirteen years ago when the Attorney General's office did a similar survey, very few Jewish officers were found at Irving Trust and Morgan. No action was taken and the two banks have since hired only a few more Jews.

Chapter Notes

1. Over half of this chapter appeared as an article, "Anti-Semitism in Banking," in The Bankers Magazine, July-August, 1977.

2. Harold E. Quinley and Charles Y. Glock, Anti-Semitism in America (New York: The Free Press 1979), p. 9.

3. This section appeared as part of an article, "The Corporate Wasp," in the Jewish Spectator, Summer, 1979.

CHAPTER IX.   THE EINSTEIN SYNDROME

In this chapter, we'll try to bring it all
together.   There is a certain system with its own
compelling logic which pushes Jews as well as other
population groups into specific ecnomic roles.   The
role of most Jews is that of socioeconomic middleman
or intellectual gladiator.   We will also be touching
upon Black, Arab, and Jewish anti-Semitism to the
degree that they are extensions of these roles.
Towards the end of this chapter we will consider
how anti-Semitic employment practices affect our
economic efficiency.

A.   Jews and Large Corporations

If you are Jewish, it is very unlikely that you
will wind up in the executive suite of a major American
corporation.   First of all, you probably will attend
a predominantly Jewish college -- part of the City
University of New York, New York University, Brandeis,
Columbia, or Washington University -- all of which
are shunned by corporate recruiters.   The chances of

such schools receiving a visit by a representative of
a large corporation are about one-third to one-fifth
as great as schools with substantially lower Jewish
enrollments. (See Chapter IV.)

But that's just the beginning. Even if a recruiter
should grace your college with his presence, according
to our alumni survey (see Chapter VII), your chances
of ending up with a major corporation are still only
one-third to one-quarter those of your gentile classmate.

This data makes for some pretty long odds. The
betting here is that a Jewish college graduate has less
than one-tenth the chance to land a job with a major
corporation than a non-Jewish college graduate. Of
course, if we were to exclude the Jewish-owned companies
among the majors, the odds would be even longer.

But getting there is only half the fun. Once
an employee of one of America's major corporations,
particularly a large New York City bank, you will
probably be steered into a "Jewish job." (See
Chapter VIII.) In fact, you were probably hired in
the first place because you had a "Jewish skill."

We found nearly every Jewish officer at the large
New York banks in non-banking positions. As we
mentioned in Chapter VIII, "All but three of the
Jewish officers we interviewed were either in computer
programming, accounting, public relations, legal work,
economic analysis, personnel work, real estate
operations, or factoring." Mainstream management
positions -- line positions in industrial companies
and national lending officer slots at commercial
banks -- are seldom open to Jewish executives. The
latter are almost invariably relegated to staff
positions on the periphery of the corporate mainstream.

Our findings are consistent with those which
the Anti-Defamation League and the American Jewish
Committee reported in earlier surveys (see Chapter
III). They add up to this: if you're Jewish,
your chances of being hired by a large corporation
are about 5 or 10% as great as those of your gentile
contemporary. And if you happen to be hired, you
will be doing "Jewish work." Just as one is accustomed
to seeing Black janitors and women secretaries, one
would expect to find Jewish computer programmers,
lawyers, and accountants. And in the case of corporate

America, what you expect is what you get.

B. Jews and Bureaucracies

As we noted in Chapter II , most of us have two
choices: we can work for a large corporate or government bureaucracy, or we can work for ourselves. Jews,
perhaps more than any other group, have opted to work
for themselves. As small business opportunities have
declined, a very high proportion of Jews turned to
the professions -- accounting, law, medicine, as well
as to computer programming, engineering, and other
technical specialties.

Stephen Isaacs stressed this point in his Jews in
American Politics:

> Most Jews believe bureaucracies to
> be especially susceptible to anti-
> Semitism, since any unfriendly
> official anywhere up the line can
> cause immense problems. When options
> are available, Jews usually opt for
> self-employment, where lineage is
> not as much of a factor as is the
> simple matter of whether one can get
> the job done -- i.e., a merit system.[1]

In steering clear of the bureaucracies, the Jews
have slipped comfortably into two traditional roles.
One is that of the professional: the person who is
hired on the basis of merit rather than certain rather
nebulous social requisites.[2] But another role has
been allocated to Jews for at least one thousand
years -- that of socioeconomic middleman.

C. The Jew as Socioeconomic Middleman

Jews have long been relegated to the role of
economic buffer between the ruling classes and the
turbulent masses. Today, when Black anti-Semitism has
become an issue, we see the Jews as a go-between,

ministering to the needs of (and occasionally ex-
ploiting) the cities' great masses of Blacks and
Hispanics. We think of these middleman occupations
as being typically Jewish -- teacher, social worker,
Legal Aid attorney, pawnshop broker, retail shopowner,
garment industry employer, and landlord.

This role is a traditional one for Jews, dating
back to medieval times, when they were even more
excluded from most occupations. This role, according
to Salo Baron et al., is a root cause of anti-Semitism:

> Like the nobility, the gentry preferred
> in many cases to have the Jews act
> as a buffer between them and the
> peasantry, so that for the oppor-
> tunity of employment and income the
> Jews assumed the role of the gentry's
> agent in the economic exploitation
> of the peasantry and in effect became
> the scapegoat of the righteous wrath
> of the peasants.[3]

This same point is made by Aviva Cantor Zuckoff: "For
centuries Jews have been programmed into certain roles
in society which they still play: the middleman, the
'oppressor surrogate,' and the scapegoat."[4]   Zuckoff
goes on to note that "the Jew functions as society's
'lightning rod' for absorbing and deflecting the rage
of oppressed groups that might otherwise be turned on
the ruling elite."[5]

Still again, Isaacs draws a parallel between the
socioeconomic role of the Jews in Europe and America:

> In Europe, the Jews served as money-
> lenders and brokers and tax collectors
> and performed chores so that the
> political and ecclesiastical rulers
> could hire armies to fight their
> wars. In America, the Jews act as
> though those same roles were com-
> pulsory, although the job descriptions
> have, of course, changed with the
> times.[6]

146

Jews have long been in the ironic position of being excluded from most economic sectors and forced into serving as economic go-betweens for the ruling classes. As such, they have been, simultaneously, the targets of anti-Semitism from both the exploiters and the exploited. As we turn now to black anti-Semitism in America, we can see a certain parallel between this phenomeonon and the earlier anti-Semitism of the eastern European peasant.

D. Black Anti-Semitism

Just as there is no single explanation for anti-Semitism, or, for that matter, prejudice of any form, so there is no single explanation for black anti-Semitism in America. We would do well to remember that Blacks, although they might feel a kinship toward Jews as fellow-sufferers, are prone to the same prejudices as their fellow Christians. However, the close economic proximity of Blacks and Jews, the "exploitive" nature of the Jewish economic role with respect to Blacks, and the Christ-like role of the Jews -- taking on the sins of all white men -- certainly explain a good part of Black anti-Semitism.

Carried to its extreme by Jews for Urban Justice, this view explicitly blames the ruling class ("empire") for black anti-Semitism and Jewish racism:

> Thus Jewish grocers and Jewish teachers
> have been both pressed by the ruling
> class -- as grocers and teachers,
> not as Jews -- to exploit and control
> Black communities. For example,
> banks, wholesalers, and great real
> estate owners have through high in-
> terest rates, high wholesale prices,
> and high rents pushed small grocers
> into charging high prices for marginal
> goods. Basically the same mechanism
> is used by the empire when it assigns
> Jewish teachers to be front-line
> controllers of Black children, and
> tries to break any effort by Jewish
> teachers to mutiny against this role.
> The result has been deep antagonism

> between the Black and the Jews
> who were forced by the ruling class
> into this deadly embrace -- and
> sometimes the emergence of anti-
> Semitism on the one side and anti-
> Black racism on the other.[7]

This deadly embrace between Blacks and Jews can be broken, then, only when the economic exploitation of both groups is broken. This view is completely consistent with our own -- that Jews have been relegated to a traditional economic role. Rabbi Arthur Hertzberg, President of the American Jewish Congress, put it very succinctly:

> ...both Jews and Blacks are marginal
> to the power structure of the United
> States. The goyish world looks at
> Jews as a pool of brains to be used
> and at Blacks as a pool of backs to
> be used. The WASP world would be
> perfectly willing to let the brains
> and the backs fight it out.[8]

From the standpoint of this book, Black anti-Semitism is virtually irrelevant, since Blacks are rarely in a position to do hiring or promoting in the corporate sector. Both Blacks and Jews are outsiders in the corporate world, and, as in the Civil Rights movement, natural allies rather than antagonists. This point will be developed further in the next chapter.

E. Arab Anti-Semitism

As many Arab leaders point out, they too, are a Semitic people, so they can hardly be accused of anti-Semitism. On the other hand, there are Jewish anti-Semites, but we know that in the case of the Arabs, it is not themselves they hate.

Another distinction often made is between anti-Zionism and anti-Semitism. "We are anti-Israel," is the refrain, "not anti-Jew." Although in some

cases that may well be true, it would still be pretty
hard to get up a minyan among the tens of thousands of
Americans employed in Saudi Arabia -- or, for that
matter, in any other Arab country.

The question here is the effect that the Arab
economic boycott of Israel has had on Jewish employment
patterns in the United States. Although numerous
instances of anti-Semitic employment requests have
been made and accommodated by American corporations,[9]
there is little hard evidence that the boycott had
had much effect in barring Jews from corporate employment. This is so mainly because Jews would have
enough trouble finding corporate employment even
without the boycott.

Perhaps construction is one area where the boycott
has been most effective. Surely such firms as Bechtel,
Ebasco, and Schlumberger are not known to go out of
their way to recruit Jews.

> Because the building industry,
> architects included, regards Jewish
> names as an embarrassment whenever
> Arabs are around, the "voluntary
> boycott" pervades this field. Some
> firms "launder" themselves of Jewish
> connections before even seeking
> business in the Arab world, and
> some carefully segregate their Jewish
> workers to projects where they are
> unlikely to meet Arab clients.[10]

F. Jewish Anti-Semitism

Although certainly there exist Jews who consider
Israel imperialistic, and there are even Jews,
particularly on the extreme political left, who may
be accused of being anti-Semitic, we will confine
our remarks to the ways in which Jewish anti-Semitism
affects Jewish employment patterns. What has been
viewed by some as apparent anti-Semitism, particularly
in large Jewish companies with WASP images, is really,
as we will see, a reaction to other's anti-Semitism,
rather than some insidious form of self-hatred.

149

Like other groups, Jews, too, can be guilty of
discrimination when they are "running the show."
Unlike other groups, however, Jews tend to turn that
discrimination inward, against themselves. Jewish-
owned organizations like the Bank of North America
(the Vogel family), CBS (William Paley) and the New
York Times (the Ochs-Sulzberger family) not only
project WASP images, but they've also earned these
images at other Jews' expense. A vivid illustration
of this practice was reported by Gay Talese in his
massive The Kingdom and the Power, a history of the
Times:

> Then in 1939 there was a story
> by Raskin that was particularly well
> liked by Raymond McCaw in the bull-
> pen, and McCaw walked over to the city
> desk to ask who had written it.
>
> "Abe Raskin," was the reply.
>
> "Put a by-line on it," McCaw said,
> and then as an afterthought, he asked,
> "What's Abe's middle initial?"
>
> "H."
>
> "Well," McCaw said, "sign it 'A.H.
> Raskin.'"
>
> McCaw's saying "sign it 'A.H.
> Raskin,'" and not "sign it 'Abraham
> Raskin'" or "'Abraham H. Raskin'"
> was interesting, because it raised
> quietly a question that would not
> have been raised aloud in The New York
> Times' newsroom. There was a feeling
> among some Jewish reporters in the
> Thirties, however reluctant they were
> to discuss it openly, that Ochs and
> Sulzberger, sensitive men, did not
> want The Times to appear "too Jewish"
> in public, and one small result of
> this was the tendency of editors to
> sign stories with initials in place
> of such names as Abraham, although,
> again, the reporters could not prove
> it and they were wise to keep this
> theory to themselves. Or it might

be a Raymond McCaw saying, without
ulterior motive, "Sign it 'A.H. Raskin'" --
as other Times editors, years later,
would sign the by-line of Abe Weiler,
a movie critic, "A.H. Weiler," and of
Abe Rosenthal, a foreign correspondent,
"A.M. Rosenthal."11

Abe Rosenthal since became the Times' first Jewish
Managing Editor and is now Executive Editor. And to
this day the name on the paper's masthead remains "A.H.
Rosenthal."

This attitude was well depicted by David
Halberstam's description of Adolph Ochs, founder of
The Times:

> He was very sensitive about being
> Jewish, which was a dominating charac-
> teristic about him and the dynasty he
> founded. They were good and respecta-
> ble German Jews at a time when the
> nation was being flooded with Jewish
> immigrants from Russia and Poland;
> the German Jews, who had seemed more
> German than the Germans in the old
> country, now if anything seemed more
> Protestant than the Protestants in
> the new. But the Eastern European
> Jews, given to beards, long hair,
> and radical political theories, did
> not fit in.... Their presence stirred
> anti-Semitism.... Ochs, good citizen
> that he was and intended to be,
> coveted the respect of the good
> people of the Gentile world. He was
> what was then called a White Jew.12

According to Halberstam, Adolph Ochs' grandson
inherited his fears along with the newspaper:

> Whatever convictions Arthur Hays
> Sulzberger held about most things

his sensitivity to anti-Semitism never
abated. Above all, he did not want
the paper to be too Jewish in tone,
and he did not want too many Jewish
executives. He, like many senior
Jewish leaders of his generation, did
not want Jews in places where they
might attract attention and controversy. In 1939 he was among a group
of Jewish leaders who urged Franklin
Roosevelt not to appoint Felix
Frankfurter to the Supreme Court,
for fear that it might increase anti-
Semitism.[13]

In addition to The New York Times and the
Washington Post, the only other significant Jewish
ownership position is the chain of newspapers held
by the Newhouse family. Isaacs noted that "The
Newhouse chain ... employs only non-Jews as editors
or publishers except for members of the immediate
Newhouse family. In fact, in 1951 when Philip
Hochstein was a directing editor for Newhouse, he
conducted a search for a new editor for the chain's
newspaper in Harrisburg, Pennsylvania, stipulating
that the editor could be neither a Jew nor a
Catholic.

Television is another area with a very substantial Jewish presence. In fact, all three major
networks were founded by Jews. As we noted in
Chapter II, Jews were often innovators and started
new enterprises, because their way was barred at
the old, established firms. But, like the Times,
the networks seek to project that same old WASP
magic.

In a rather perceptive study of the industry,
Les Brown observed that the heads of CBS, NBC, and
ABC "appear to have taken such extreme caution
against fueling the idea of 'Jewish networks' that
they have in fact discriminated against Jewish
executives who might have qualified for leadership
posts.[15] "In terms of Jews," said Isaacs, "television
news is still a-Semitic, even though -- or perhaps
because -- the networks are owned and managed largely
by Jews ... that no Jew could be an 'anchor man'
raises the suspicion that the networks have bent
backwards to avoid any suggestion of being 'Jewish'

as well as to purvey a comforting image to the over-whelmingly WASP audience."[16]

Arthur Liebman observed the same phenomenon in investment banking. "Here Jewish houses will for purposes of business, hire or appoint Christian partners, but Christian investment firms do not tend to acquire Jewish partners."[17] For example, just check out the pedigree of the partners at Lehman Brothers with that of the Brown Brothers Harriman partners.

While Jewish employers are often reluctant to hire too many Jews, this reluctance stems mainly from a fear of what the gentile world will think rather than any degree of anti-Semitism, or self-hatred. These employers are, in effect, saying: "It's bad enough we have to be Jewish; we have to rub their noses in it?" What might otherwise pass for Jewish anti-Semitism is merely that old familiar Jewish fear of calling too much attention to oneself.

We will sum up the basic message of this section by quoting Aviva Cantor Zuckoff once again:

> Jews are constantly looking to the goyim for approval; the main question always is "what will the goyim say?" This is reflected in Jews' striving to prove how well they fit into their view of society."[18]

G.   The Jew as an Intellectual Gladiator

Americans have a way of getting things done. Take dirty work. We used to foist that off on slaves, then immigrants. More recently we've got women and members of various minority groups to do the most demeaning, low-paid work in our society.

In this section we'll be discussing how we get our brain work done. How do we fill all those slots for scientists, computer programmers, playwrights, and college professors? Turns out, these positions are often filled by Jews. Just as secretarial work is "women's work," we define any job demanding considerable intelligence as "Jewish work." The principle's the same, though the pay is often better.

Gladiators, whether Roman slaves, Spanish bull-fighters, or American Black athletes, have long ful-filled a specific social role. Not only did they entertain, but they also did something the rest of us could not do nearly as well, if at all. Historically, we have just sat back to watch the gladiators go about their business.

American Jews, in a sense, are fulfilling their historic mission as intellectual gladiators. Mordechai played that role for the King of Persia, as did the court Jews through the intervening years. Henry Kissinger was a hired brain who sold himself to those people who could afford his price in terms of money and power.

You seldom find a Jew at the top of any organi-zation, be it a bank, a large corporation, a uni-versity, or, for that matter, a country. In fact, the only countries run by Jews in modern times besides Israel have been France (Leon Blum before World War II and Pierre Mendes-France in the mid-fifties) and Austria (Bruno Kreisky is the current Prime Minister).

To call someone an "Einstein" means not just someone super-smart, but someone who has a particular type of intelligence -- very scientific, abstract, capable of doing all kinds of esoteric calculations. In fact, it seems, Jews are particularly well-suited for this kind of work.

The first time we came across the term, "the Einstein Syndrome," was in a 1969 Los Angeles Times story by Jack Smith.[19] About a decade later Ira Gissen observed "Many industries have for years held to the belief that 'there are some jobs Jews are good for.'"[20]

The Jews have certainly supplied the country with more than their proportionate share of scientists, college professors, poets, composers, playwrights, novelists, psychiatrists, and other intellectual types. And even oil billionaires like the Hunt brothers might seek out smart Jewish lawyers and accountants. If you need to get the job done, hire a smart Jew.

Go up to the data processing department at Chase Manhattan Bank. You'll see a group of people who are definitely not banking types -- beards, ill-fitting clothing, even funny accents. No, they're not hippies, It turns out that although the large New York banks have relatively few Jewish officers, over half the bank computer programmers are Jewish.

The Jewish experience in academia wasn't too different from that in banking. There seems to be no shortage of Jewish college professors, yet they are virtually absent from college administration. Nationwide, about ten per cent of all professors are Jewish, but only a handful of college presidents are Jewish. After the presidents of Brandeis, Yeshiva, a few units of the City University of New York, and another few public universities in New York and New Jersey, there is only a sprinkling of Jewish college presidents and administrators around the country.[21]

The Jewish academic, then, qualifies as an intellectual gladiator. He can teach and do research, but keep him away from that "A" building. And just as the athletic spectator comes away with the impression that Blacks play strong, if not dominant, roles in major league sports, so also does the academic observer see all those Jewish intellectual stars.

The atomic bomb project was entrusted to the likes of Albert Einstein, Robert Oppenheimer, and Edward Teller, but the universities they were associated with had almost no Jewish administrators. The Jews could give nearly half the large donations and staff the political braintrusts, but no Jew has even placed his name in contention for a major party presidential nomination. Clearly, American Jews know their place.

Jews, of course, fill other economic slots besides those labelled "intellectual." The movie moguls, garment manufacturers, civil servants, and the school teachers do not rank too highly among the nation's deep thinkers. In general, then, the Jews will take whatever jobs they can get. "Get" is the operative word, implying that there's someone giving out the jobs one tries to get.

Someone is giving out jobs -- Jewish jobs, Black jobs, jobs for Italians, Poles, WASPs, or whatever. What is important in America is that we define work by who does it. Brain work is Jewish work. Janitorial work is for Blacks. Secretarial positions are reserved

for women. And Black women make especially good
domestics.

Whether we as a society are at fault for this
state of affairs or whether the nation's opinion
leaders (many of whom, ironically, are Jewish), we
have got to change the way we look both at jobs and
at the people who do them. "Black is beautiful" and
sexual consciousness-raising are two important steps.
But in the end, we all need to be liberated -- from
our own oppressive prejudices.

H. Anti-Semitism and Economic Efficiency[22]

No society can operate at full efficiency if
jobs are allocated on any basis other than merit. For
centuries we have arbitrarily determined that certain
types of work should be performed by women, or
Blacks, or Italians, or Jews. In the more technical
fields, it was recognized that these prejudices
deprived society of the services of many talented
people. But corporate management continues to be
the special preserve of WASPs, with small quotas
for Blacks, Hispanics, and women. This hiring policy
not only keeps the door shut on Jews and other
"ethnics," but it ignores merit as a hiring criterion.

If, by extension, the quota system were carried
to its logical conclusion, there would be a quota
for everyone -- Jews, Italians, hyphenated Americans
of every extraction, and even for the last of the
endangered species, the WASP. One would not need to
be an efficiency expert to see how this system would
wreak havoc with our economy. We might note, in
passing, that Jews have never fared well with quota
systems.

One might speculate that the decline in America's
economic preeminence (and England's earlier decline)
was due to a relatively rigid socioeconomic structure
that allocated jobs on the basis of social connections
rather than ability. America's slow economic growth
might be traced to an ossified cadre of corporate
managers whose bland conservatism appears to be their
sole qualification.

What is bad for the Jews -- and for women,
Blacks, Hispanics, and "ethnics" -- is bad for America.
It is in everyone's best interest to end employment

156

discrimination, if only because it seriously weakens our economic efficiency. The question that remains is what can be done to fight this discrimination?

Chapter Notes

1. Stephen Isaacs, Jews and American Politics (Garden City, N.Y.: Doubleday & Co., 1974), p. 33. See also Arthur Liebman, Jews and the Left (New York: John Wiley & Sons, 1979), p. 441.

2. See Nathan Glazer and Daniel Moynihan, Beyond the Melting Pot (Cambridge, Mass: The M.I.T. Press, 1970), 2nd Ed., p. 148.

3. Salo W. Baron, Arcadius Kahan, and others (Edited by Nachum Gross) , Economic History of the Jews (New York: Schocken Books, 1975), p. 71.

4. Aviva Cantor Zuckoff, "The Oppression of America's Jews," in Jack Nusan Porter and Peter Dreier, etds., Jewish Radicalism (New York: Grove Press, 1973), p. 30.

5. Zuckoff, op. cit., page 31

6. Isaacs, op. cit., page 13.

7. Jews for Urban Justice, in Jack Nusan Porter and Peter Dreier, eds., Jewish Radicalism (New York: Grove Press, 1973), p. 30.

8. Isaacs, op. cit., p. 166.

9. These cases are extensively documented by the American Jewish Congress in Boycott Report, which has been issued nine times a year since 1977.

10. Walter H. Nelson and Terence Prittie, The Economic War Against The Jews (New York: Random House, 1977), p. 82.

11. Gay Talese, The Kingdom and the Power (New York: World Publishing Company, 1966), pages 59 and 60.

12. David Halberstam, The Powers That Be (New York: Dell Publishing Co., 1979), p. 293.

13. Halberstam, op. cit., p. 306.

14. Isaacs, op. cit., p. 49.

15. Les Brown, Television, The Business Behind the Box (New York: Harcourt Brace Jovanovich, 1968), p. 216.

16. Isaacs, op. cit., p. 46.

17. Liebman, op. cit., p. 606.

18. Zuckoff, op cit., pp. 34 35.

19. Jack Smith, "Club Barriers Thwart Careers, Study Discloses," Los Angeles Times, July 3, 1969.

20. Ira Gissen, ed., "A Study of Jewish Employment Patterns in the Big Six Oil Company Headquarters," Rights, Summer, 1978.

21. Questionnaires were sent to 520 colleges throughout the country; replies were received from 215 schools. Follow-up letters were sent to presidents who indicated they were Jewish asking if they knew of other schools with Jewish presidents. Of the more than 2,000 four-year colleges in the country, we found 41 with Jewish presidents. Twenty-one of the 41 were located in New York, New Jersey, Pennsylvania, and California.

22. Most of this section appeared in the Jewish Spectator, Summer, 1979.

CHAPTER X.   WHAT CAN BE DONE?

A.   Introduction

     The Jews have been kicked around for some 2,000
years , and, since the Holocaust, millions have been
saying that famous line of Peter Finch's in the movie,
Network, "I'm mad as hell, and I'm not going to take
it any more!"   Or in the succinct two-word motto of
the Jewish Defense League, "Never again!"

     After what Hitler did to the Jews, there can
never again be the most Christian-like response of
turning the other cheek.   The creation of the State
of Israel has obviously stirred tremendous opposition,
particularly in the Arab world.   But when six million
Jews had been slaughtered, the entire world just looked
the other way.   Now, at least, there's one country
that will take in the Jews.   And as secure as America's
Jews feel -- and as secure as German's Jews once
felt -- we would do well to recall the observation
of Feliks Gross: "The Jews have been expelled by
every host nation."

Even today in Poland the Jewish community of just six thousand, mostly elderly people, is being blamed for at least some of the nation's economic and political woes in a way reminiscent of the blame heaped upon the three million Jews who lived there before World War II. But, of course, in the words of Sinclair Lewis, "It Can't Happen Here."

In a similar vein, however reprehensible the tactics of the Jewish Defense League, one cannot question their basic premise -- if "they" know we won't fight back, they'll keep kicking us around. The only question, then, is how to fight back. And that is what this chapter is about.

From the time of the Maccabees to the uprising of the Warsaw ghetto, how many times have the Jews fought back? Defenselessness was the only defense, as Aviva Cantor Zuckoff points out:

> Two thousand years of oppression
> have taught Jews that those who
> survived were those who hid in
> the cellar or took to their feet
> in time -- not those who fought.
> Jewish defenselessness is among the
> most dehumanizing aspects of Jewish
> oppression -- and the most dangerous.
> For it is precisely this defenseless-
> ness that provokes and encourages
> attack. Jews will not riot and
> the goyim count on this. We do
> not know what would have happened
> had German Jews rioted against
> Hitler before or just when he came
> to power; but we do know the Nazis
> counted on the fact that they would
> not do so.[1]

B. The Big Three: The American Jewish Committee, the Anti-Defamation League, and the American Jewish Congress

We have cited various studies by these groups, particularly in Chapter III, and have noted their strong defense of Israel and their consistent

162

opposition to the Arab economic boycott. Unfortunately, they have a rather mixed record in fighting anti-Semitism in large American corporations. Elias Cooper, writing in the American Zionist, called for an entirely new "political" approach to anti-Semitism:

> The most important thing is to make it well understood that anti-Semitism does not pay. If our defense organizations had concentrated on this task, instead of protesting against Christmas stamps, there would never have been any need for Jewish vigilantism.... Nevertheless, the JDL approached the problem as a political one, which is a step in the right direction, even if its placards are odious. No amount of criticism of the JDL will nullify the revolution of contempt that is brewing in the Jewish community against the major Jewish organizations. These organizations cannot justify their existence -- and expenditure of the community's funds -- by issuing innocent 'analyses.' They are needed for political action.[2]

The Executive Suite Program of the American Jewish Committee attempts what amounts to consciousness-raising among the top executives. Burt Siegel, who has directed the program for more than a year, told us that his "efforts will have a subtle kind of effect" rather than directly measurable results.

Siegel and another member of his group meet with a top corporate executive, often the personnel director. Typically, the AJC representatives note that as far as they could determine, x number of Jews are employed as executives of the company, and inquire whether any further information is available. "The first response of the corporate officer is likely to be that they have no idea who is Jewish and they, therefore, have no idea how many Jews are in the corporation."[3] If the number of Jews appears to be low, then "We could ask that they supply us with their college recruitment schedule, as does AT&T, for distribution to AJC area offices which can share them with local contacts."[4]

The perception of large corporations in the Jewish community is also stressed. "College recruiters should be in touch with Hillel Foundations to inform them of their campus schedule. This will be a strong 'signal' to the Jewish students that the corporation is serious about non-discrimination with respect to Jews. We should make sure they recruit on campuses with significant Jewish enrollment."[5]

Virtually no major corporations have avoided meeting with Siegel or his predecessors, Israel Laster and Sam Freedman. But what happens when, after several meetings, there are still only a handful of Jews in executive positions? Whether the AJC or any other Jewish organization, when directly confronted with a judenrein corporate policy, will be willing to go to court, impose economic sanctions, or even go public with the information, is something we still don't know.

We know that when Israel's security is threatened, the Big Three will go on full red alert. If the Kremlin steps up its repression of Soviet Jewry, the full political forces of the Jewish community are mobilized. We would ask that American Jews be afforded the same protection.

C. A Step-By-Step Approach

There are several companies which are almost overtly anti-Semitic -- Morgan Guaranty, Irving Trust, Johnson & Johnson -- which we should go after. Their recruiters avoid schools with large Jewish enrollments, they hire as few Jews as possible, and those few are guided into "Jewish jobs" and rarely promoted. By doing this, they are breaking the law.

We need to go to their personnel officers and tell them: (1) According to our figures, you have x number of Jews in such and such positions -- is this accurate? (2) We suggest you recruit at schools with high Jewish enrollments and we will aid you in this effort. (3) Your recruitment of executive trainees will be monitored. (4) If your recruitment continues to be biased against Jewish applicants we will take you to court.

164

We must go after the worst offenders first. We must insist on prompt remedial action. We must be prepared to take legal action if it appears that anti-Semitic hiring patterns persist.

One problem which was stressed by Joe Robison, Assistant General Counsel for the American Jewish Congress, is to find a person willing to sue a company for employment discrimination. We spoke to several officials of the Anti-Defamation League from various parts of the country, and nearly all cited this difficulty. From the time a case is heard, often by the state human rights commission, and, if merit is found, by the courts, years have elapsed, and the plaintiff has either got discouraged, or settled out of court. In Chapter III , Section E, this was illustrated by the Standard Oil of California case.

Unlike Blacks and women, who have successfully pressed scores of employment discrimination cases, Jews have been singularly reluctant to sue. Perhaps one reason is the difficulty of proving a pattern of discrimination -- a difficulty that obviously does not exist with respect to women and blacks. Jews don't tend to stand out as much in a crowd.

Our suspicion is that the legal approach will be successful only if a substantial case can be built and prosecuted against a leading discriminator -- a Morgan Guaranty or a Johnson & Johnson -- on the basis of massive evidence, perhaps along the lines that we have presented. It would be important for not just one, but several individuals to bring suit against such firms.

It's easy to sit back and say, "This proves nothing; so what if we don't have so many Jews working here?" But from there, it is an easy step to , "Let's not do anything about it." And to do nothing about injustice, to let things go on as they have been going on for years -- that is the real objective of those who are running things. In other words, "until you can come up with a perfect case -- and we'll make sure you never do -- then don't come around here bitching about discrimination."

D.   Direct Action

Legal action, while the preferred approach, is usually time consuming and inconclusive. A boycott of a company's products is another possibility. Usually a company that discriminates against Jews discriminates against other groups as well. As we noted in Chapter VI, Section D, most corporate officials tend to hire people with whom they're compatible, people just like themselves. Since the vast majority of those people happen to be WASP males, it is understandable that WASP male applicants are most likely to be hired.

A boycott, then, could enlist the support of other groups as well as Jews. When the United Farm Workers union (whose membership is virtually all Mexican-American) boycotted iceberg lettuce and Gallo wine, those who stopped buying these products were mainly big city liberals (almost none of whom were Mexican-American). Were the Jews to make common cause with women's organizations, civil rights groups, and various ethnic organizations, there would be much greater leverage.

In this account of a demonstration reported in the Jewish Press, we have perhaps the only instance when American Jews took direct action against a discriminatory employer:

> Hundreds of passersby watched anxiously as a dozen young men, wearing yarmulkas, picketed the Anchor Savings Bank...in the predominantly Jewish section of Boro Park, protesting alleged discrimination in the hiring practices at the bank.
>
> The pickets demanded "Jobs for Jews," "Take your money out," "No Jobs -- No Deposits," as they marched peacefully for about an hour under the watchful eyes of the police....
>
> Housewives and storekeepers... resented the fact that the bank was taking advantage of their location

and refused to hire more Jews than
they had. Out of a total of approximately 150 personnel, Anchor
Savings Bank had admitted to having
about six or seven Jewish employees,...

Two spokesmen for the bank,
identified as Mr. Coopersmith and
Mr. Landau, tried to convince a
group of about 50 that the reason
there were so few Jewish employees
at Anchor Savings was due to the
fact that there were no applicants.
They handed out application forms....

Mr. Landau said that any qualified
person could apply, providing they
didn't have 'those curly locks [on
the side of their face].'[6]

The demonstration just described is just a small-
scale scenarious of what might interestingly be tried.
Imagine if depositors suddenly started conspicuously
withdrawing their money from one of New York's leading
banks. Because banks are required to keep a certain
percentage of their deposits on reserve -- and they
seldom carry excess reserves -- a sudden massive with-
drawal could wreak havoc. Just the threat of such an
action might precipitate massive withdrawals by panicky
depositors afraid the bank is failing.

Just as companies are responsive to the threat
of a strike, perhaps the banks, too, might respond
similarly to the threat of mass withdrawals. It
goes without saying that such threats must never be
idly made. We would have to know that discrimination
was blatant and that the bank's officials had refused
to take the necessary remedial measures. But we would
also have to know that there were thousands of
depositors who would be willing to withdraw their
money. And this would require a great deal of
organizing.

E. The Corporate System

Basically we are condemning discrimination against
all groups. What is needed is an entire overhaul of

the corporate hiring system. For too long people have been hired for the wrong jobs for the wrong reasons. Not only is this patently unfair, but it results in a vast misallocation of labor.

There is a huge and growing concentration of wealth in this country, and the control of the economy is in the hands of a very few people. These people should be called to account for a lot of society's injustices, not the least of which is their own power. At a minimum, it can be said that that power has not been exercised on behalf of equal employment opportunity. And it is quite possible that that concentration of power is largely responsible for much of the employment discrimination in America today.

F. Conclusion

What can be done? One thing which Jews should stop doing is being such good Christians; whatever the religious merits of turning the other cheek, it won't get anyone a job. Yet one young Jewish executive trainee told us, "People don't want to think about anti-Semitism. Why bring up the topic? What good will come of it? If those in a position to hire and promote become conscious of Jews as such, perhaps they will discriminate. Why stir them up?"

In testimony before the U.S. Congressional Committee on Education and Labor (January 22, 1976), ADL spokesman Ira Gissen noted that the federal, state, and local equal opportunity agencies are not effectively enforcing "the bans against religious discrimination." We believe it is crucial for Jews to bring their complaints to the appropriate authorities, regardless of who will be stirred up.

To make waves would admittedly put some people in a difficult position. For example, someone whose progress up the corporate ladder has been slower than he had hoped would be reluctant to make a formal complaint and become known as a troublemaker. Many executives told us they can never be sure if their being Jewish has held them back, even though very few other Jews in their corporations occupy senior positions. It would somehow be unseemly for a Jewish officer, even at Morgan Guaranty or Irving Trust (neither of which provide very hospitable environments for their Jewish employees), to lodge any complaint whatsoever. In fact, last year, not a murmur of protest was raised when Morgan held its officers' picnic on <u>Yom Kippur</u>.

The ADL, the AJC, and other Jewish organizations have exerted some pressure on many firms to hire more Jews. This effort, however, has been applied infrequently, inconsistently, and to only a minimal effect. Firms with a history of Jewish underrepresentation continue excluding Jewish applicants without even a reprimand from the Jewish establishment.

We have, then, a picture of laxity both on the part of governmental agencies and the Jewish ones as well. To this add Jewish executives' marked and understandable reticence to make waves. Furthermore, the vast body of Jewish college graduates who somehow don't get offers of corporate employment remain unmobilized, indeed unaware of how systematic and typical this exclusion is.

We believe that until corporate jobs are allocated on the basis of merit, not only will America operate well below optimal efficiency, but Jewish college graduates will remain at the short end of the stick. It would probably be counterproductive for Jews to ask for job quotas. However, one way to judge corporate sincerity is to look at the hiring record of minorities, including Jews. We must demand that all jobs in America be filled solely on the basis of merit. This would not only be good for the Jews, but good for America as well.

Chapter Notes

1. Aviva Cantor Zuckoff, "The Oppression of America's Jews," in Jack Nusan Porter and Peter Dreier, eds., Jewish Radicalism (New York: Grove Press, 1973), pp. 33 - 34.

2. Elias Cooper, "The Jewish Condition in America," The American Zionist, September 1969, p. 25.

3. Burt A. Siegel, Manual of Procedures: New York Regional Task Force on Executive Suite (New York: American Jewish Committee October 22, 1981) (mimeo), p. 2.

4. Siegel, op. cit., p. 3.

5. Siegel, op. cit., p. 2.

6. Chaim Lipshitz and Judah Schwartz, "Picket Anchor Savings Bank Demand More Jobs For Jews," The Jewish Press, May 16, 1969.

7. This section was part of our article, "The Corporate WASP," which appeared in the Jewish Spectator Summer, 1979, p. 32.

APPENDIX

There are three sections included in this appendix.
The data of Section A provides the basis for Chapter
IV's analysis. The formula for deriving the probability
estimates used in Chapter V is explained in Section B.
Finally, a list of Jewish and Christian names used in
the sampling of corporate executives used in Chapter
VII is presented in Section C.

A. Colleges Participating in Survey

The colleges participating in our survey are found
in Table I below. We have also indicated the percentage
of enrollment that is Jewish for each college. As
might be expected, most of the heavily Jewish schools
are in the New York area.

171

TABLE I

JEWISH ENROLLMENTS OF COLLEGES PARTICIPATING IN SURVEY
1972-1974

College	% of Undergraduate Enrollment that is Jewish
Alabama	
Auburn University	0.4%
University of Alabama	1.3
Arizona	
Arizona State University	6.6
University of Arizona	5.0
Arkansas	
University of Arkansas	4.0
California	
Stanford	7.5
University of California - Berkeley	19.5
UCLA	29.0
University of San Francisco	0.8
University of Southern California	10.0
Colorado	
University of Colorado	5.7
University of Denver	15.1
Connecticut	
Eastern Connecticut State College	10.0
Fairfield University	1.0
University of Bridgeport	33.3
University of Connecticut	13.5
Wesleyan University	33.0
Yale University	32.5

TABLE I -- Continued

College	% of Undergraduate Enrollment that is Jewish
Delaware	
University of Delaware	5.5%
District of Columbia	
George Washington University	7.2
Georgetown University	12.4
Florida	
Florida A & M	4.0
Florida State University	4.7
University of Florida	8.4
University of Miami	31.5
Georgia	
Emory University	25.0
Georgia State University	1.9
University of Georgia	3.9
Idaho	
University of Idaho	
Illinois	
Bradley University	5.0
De Paul University	2.0
Loyola of Chicago	5.4
Northwestern University	15.0
Southern Illinois University	9.0
University of Chicago	27.5
University of Illinois	10.6

TABLE I -- Continued

College	% of Undergraduate Enrollment that is Jewish
Indiana	
Ball State University	4.0%
Butler University	0.4
De Pauw	0.5
Notre Dame University	0.2
Purdue University	1.9
University of Indiana	3.0
Iowa	
Drake University	9.1
Grinnell College	10.5
Iowa State University	0.3
Parsons College	---*
University of Iowa	3.5
Kansas	
University of Kansas	3.0
Kentucky	
University of Kentucky	1.3
Louisiana	
Loyola of New Orleans	2.0
Louisiana State University	1.4
Tulane University	9.8
Maine	
Bates College	3.0
Bowdoin College	3.0
University of Maine	2.5

TABLE I -- Continued

College	% of Undergraduate Enrollment that is Jewish
Maryland	
Johns Hopkins University	32.5%
University of Maryland	13.0
Massachusetts	
Amherst College	14.0
Babson College	25.0
Boston College	2.9
Boston University	38.1
Brandeis University	60.0
Harvard University	25.0
Northeastern University	10.0
Tufts University	10.0
Michigan	
Central Michigan University	0.3
Ferris State University	3.0
Michigan State University	5.4
University of Detroit	3.0
University of Michigan	17.8
Minnesota	
University of Minnesota	4.5
Mississippi	
Mississippi State University	1.0
University of Mississippi	1.0
Missouri	
St. Louis University	2.8
University of Missouri	6.5
Washington University	40.0

TABLE I -- Continued

College	% of Undergraduate Enrollment that is Jewish
Montana	
Carroll College	0.5%
University of Montana	2.0
Nebraska	
Creighton University	2.3
New Hampshire	
Dartmouth College	8.8
University of New Hampshire	4.0
New Jersey	
Drew College	8.0
Farleigh Dickinson University	25.5
Princeton University	20.0
Rutgers University	29.0
Seton Hall University	15.0
Upsala College	11.0
New Mexico	
University of New Mexico	1.0
New York	
Alfred University	7.8
Colgate University	7.0
Columbia University	32.5
City University of New York (CUNY)	
Baruch College	47.5
Brooklyn College	65.0
City College	31.3
Hunter College	50.0
Lehman College	52.5
Queens College	50.0

TABLE I -- Continued

College	% of Undergraduate Enrollment that is Jewish
City University of New York (cont'd)	
Richmond College	25.0%
York College	35.0
Cornell University	27.8
Fordham University	10.0
Hofstra College	43.5
New York University	40.0
State University of New York (SUNY)	
at Albany	25.0
at Buffalo	20.2
Syracuse University	35.0
Yeshiva University	98.0

North Carolina

Davidson University	0.2
Duke University	0.0
Methodist College	10.0
North Carolina State University	1.0
University of North Carolina	3.5
Wake Forrest University	1.0

North Dakota

University of North Dakota	0.1

Ohio

Bowling Green University	1.0
Case-Western Reserve University	12.4
Central State University	0.8
Cleveland State University	2.6
Denison College	1.9
Kent State University	8.6
Miami University	8.0
Ohio State University	8.5
University of Akron	4.0
University of Cincinnati	6.9
University of Dayton	2.0
University of Toledo	2.0
Youngstown State University	3.0

TABLE I -- Continued

College	% of Undergraduate Enrollment that is Jewish
Oklahoma	
Oklahoma State University	2.0%
University of Oklahoma	2.8
Oregon	
University of Oregon	3.9
Pennsylvania	
Bucknell University	6.0
Carnegie-Mellon University	20.0
Franklin & Marshall College	22.0
Gettysburg College	2.7
Lafayette College	17.5
Muhlenberg College	18.0
Penn State University	7.0
Susquehanna College	1.0
Temple University	32.5
University of Pennsylvania	40.0
University of Pittsburgh	10.0
Rhode Island	
Brown University	22.5
University of Rhode Island	8.8
South Carolina	
The Citadel College	2.9
Clemson University	0.5
Furman University	2.0
University of South Carolina	1.9
South Dakota	
University of South Dakota	0.8

TABLE I -- Continued

College	% of Undergraduate Enrollment that is Jewish
Tennessee	
University of Tennessee	1.0%
Vanderbilt University	5.0
Texas	
Abilene Christian College	0.0
Baylor University	0.3
Hardin-Simmons College	0.0
Rice University	0.5
Southern Methodist University	0.5
Texas Christian University	0.6
Texas Lutheran College	0.5
University of Houston	3.1
University of Texas	6.3
Utah	
Brigham Young University	0.2
University of Utah	1.0
Utah State University	0.5
Vermont	
University of Vermont	5.5
Virginia	
University of Richmond	3.6
University of Virginia	4.0
Washington	
University of Washington	2.8

TABLE I -- Continued

College	% of Undergraduate Enrollment that is Jewish
West Virginia	
University of West Virginia	1.8%
Wisconsin	
Marquette University	3.7
University of Wisconsin	12.2

* College closed (bankrupt)

B. Calculation of Probability Estimates

All of the probability estimates made in Chapter V are based on this formula:

$$(1) \quad P(x) \quad \frac{\binom{J}{x}\binom{N-J}{n-x}}{\binom{N}{n}}$$

In our case there are 170 colleges (N = 170), 21 of which are Jewish (J = 21). Thus, the non-Jewish colleges (N-J) = 149.

We want to find the probability (P) of a corporation visiting a certain number of schools (n), but randomly selecting only a given number of Jewish schools (x). Since the number of schools visited is n, and the number of Jewish schools visited is x, the number of non-Jewish schools visited is n-x.

Say, the number of schools visited is 20 (n = 20), what is the probability that if the schools are selected randomly (with respect to religion), only two would be Jewish? We could substitute the values of each of the variables in equation (1) to obtain equation (2):

$$(2) \quad P(2) \quad \frac{\binom{21}{2}\binom{170-21}{20-2}}{\binom{170}{20}}, \quad \text{which becomes: } (3) \frac{\binom{21}{2}\binom{149}{18}}{\binom{170}{20}},$$

which may be stated as:

$$(4) \quad \frac{\frac{21!}{2!} \times \frac{149!}{18!}}{\frac{170!}{20!}}.$$

These factorials may be restated: (5)

$$\frac{\left(\frac{21 \times 20}{2 \times 1}\right)\left(\frac{149 \times 148 \times 147 \ldots \times 132}{18 \times 17 \times 16 \ldots \times 1}\right)}{\left(\frac{170 \times 169 \times 168 \ldots \times 151}{20 \times 19 \times 18 \ldots \times 1}\right)}$$

This massive fraction finally reduces to P(2)   .2853.

C. Names of Jewish and Christian Executives

Table II below lists the names of the Jewish and Christian executives, which we used in the sampling described in Chapter VI. The Jewish names are typically Jewish and frankly, we doubt if any Christians have changed their names to any of those listed in Table IIA. We tried to pick Christian names (shown in Table IIB) to which few Jews would have switched.

TABLE IIA

Names of Jewish Executives

Aaronson	Farber	Haber	Levin
Abramowitz	Fein	Haberman	Levine
Abramson	Feinberg	Halperin	Levinsky
Aronoff	Feinbloom	Halpern	Levinson
Aronowitz	Feinstein	Hirschberg	Levy
	Feldman	Hirschfield	Lipsky
Berger	Feldstein	Hirschhorn	Lipstein
Berkowitz	Fenster	Hochberg	Lowenstein
Bernstein	Finkelstein	Hochenberger	
Bloom	Fried	Hochfeld	Marcus
Bloomberg	Friedberg	Hochfelder	Margolis
Bluestein	Friedland	Hochman	Margulies
Blum	Friedlander		Markowitz
Blumberg	Friedman	Jaffe	
Blumenthal			Pincus
Burstein	Gold	Kahn	
	Goldberg	Kaplan	Rabinowitz
Cahn	Goldberger	Kaplow	Rosen
Cantor	Golden	Katz	Rosenbaum
Cohen	Goldfarb	Katzman	Rosenberg
Cohn	Goldman	Korn	Rosenfeld
Cooperman	Goldstein	Kornblum	Rosenthal
	Greenberg	Kotler	Rothenberg
Dubin	Gross	Kravitz	Rothfeld
	Grossman	Krinsky	Rothman
Edelman			Rothstein
Edelson			Rubin
Edelstein			
Epstein			

Sandler
Schwartz
Schwarz
Shapiro
Shindler
Silverstein
Steinberg
Sternbach
Sussman

Tannenbaum
Teisch
Teitelbaum

Wasserman
Weinberg
Weinberger
Weinstein
Weintraub
Weisberg
Wishnick

TABLE IIB

Names of Christian Executives

Abbott	Higgins	Parsons
Abernathy	Hough	Pearce
Abernethy	Houghton	Peterson
Acheson	Hoyt	Pierce
Adams	Hubbard	
Ames		Quick
Appleby	Ives	
Applegate	Ivey	Savage
Atkinson		Scarborough
	Jansen	Schmidt
Barber	Jeffers	Seaman
Bird	Jennings	Standish
Blanchard		Strickland
Bowen	Kates	Stroud
Bowers	Kolb	Stryker
Bullock		Sutherland
Bundy	Lacy	Swenson
Burgess	Laird	Swett
	Lange	
Cain	Larsen	Talbot
Carlisle		Talbott
Child	MacDonald	Tatum
Childs	Madden	Terrell
Chisholm	MnClean	Thorne
Christensen	McCleod	Thornton
	McCormick	Thurber
Dahl	McCoy	Thurston
Drake	McCullough	Trump
	McNally	Turnbull
Edmondson	Moorehead	Tyson
Erickson	Morrhead	
	Morrow	Ulrich
Fitzgerald		Underwood
Flowers	Nichols	Upton
Foote	Nicholson	
Foss	Nielsen	Van Voorhis
		Veale
Galbraith	Olmstead	Verner
Galbreath	Olmsted	Vinson
Galvin	Olsen	
Gamble	Olson	Watts
Gibbons		Worthington
Gibbs		
Gilchrist		Yost
Griswold		

ABOUT THE AUTHORS

Stephen L. Slavin received his Ph.D. in economics from New York University and is the author of numerous articles on economics and politics that have appeared in scholarly journals and newspapers. He has taught for 16 years at variuos colleges in the New York area including Brooklyn College, New York Institute of Technology, St. Francis College, and Union College. He plans to enter the free agent draft this fall and pursue a major league baseball career.

Mary A. Pradt earned her B.S. and M.S. degrees and her Phi Beta Kappa key at Columbia University. For ten years a reference librarian with the Brooklyn Public Library, she is now a research librarian in editorial services with Time, Inc. Her nonfiction articles have appeared in a variety of publications from newspapers to trade journals and consumer magazines. Ms. Pradt is currently immersed in research on the history of Downtown Brooklyn and in photographing the Brooklyn Bridge under various lighting conditions, from the Brooklyn side.